To my dearest Jane

love you,

ONWARD
AND
UPWARD

Jim Neglia

authorHOUSE®

AuthorHouse™
1663 Liberty Drive
Bloomington, IN 47403
www.authorhouse.com
Phone: 1-800-839-8640

Published by AuthorHouse 12/13/2012

ISBN: 978-1-4772-9898-5 (sc)
ISBN: 978-1-4772-9897-8 (hc)
ISBN: 978-1-4772-9927-2 (e)

Library of Congress Control Number: 2012923491

*"There is only one success—to be able to
spend your life in your own way."*

—Christopher Morley

For as long as I can remember, I've wanted to be a professional musician. I began my quest hoping beyond hope that my desire alone would be enough to magically propel me to stardom. I soon learned that there are no shortcuts to success, no magic wands to wave; and that my desire was just the tip of the iceberg of what was actually needed. Therefore I changed my approach. I began to settle into a groove that took me on a journey of unparalleled proportions. The journey began by spending countless hours in an eight feet by eight feet practice room for up to ten hours a day, determined to sharpen my skills as a budding percussionist. The beginning years were extremely crucial: I felt it was either sink or swim. It was imperative that my dedication take root and ultimately evolve into my desired profession.

All the hard work, sweat, tears, anxiety, passion, and love ultimately paid off. Years later, I found myself performing with wonderful orchestras and chamber groups, both in the United States and throughout Europe. I had realized an unimaginable goal.

Many years later, I focused my energy on the next stages in my career: contracting. I saw firsthand, from the perspective of the musician, what it takes to be a successful contractor. Focusing on productions, presentations, preparations, and details seemed a logical starting place.

It was during my early performance days that I found myself fascinated by seeing how productions unfolded before my eyes. I thought to myself, *Someone had to hire the musicians, work with the union, prepare payroll, and be accountable for the day's events.* The more I learned, the more I wanted that person to be me. It was during this transition period from musician to producer that I began keeping detailed notes on how I could best succeed. I also took notes on many other topics, some of which I have included in the pages to come. All the while, I kept my performance chops up to snuff.

More time passed, and I found myself sifting through endless pages of notes, stories, and thoughts I had jotted down over the years. There were such a wide variety of offerings; I knew I needed to begin organizing my thoughts more carefully. In doing so, I was able to choose some of the more ridiculous, interesting, sad, scary, absurd, but hopefully mostly entertaining situations to share with you.

There were many people responsible for nurturing, prodding, and pushing me to offer these stories. They knew exactly when the support was needed the most. These are the same people who, years before, had pushed me to work harder on the music I was preparing. They are the same people who picked me up from the practice room floor when I had fallen asleep from exhaustion. They are the people who helped push me beyond the limits of the normal, and they showed me how to achieve the impossible. These are the people who have helped make my life as successful as it could be. I wish to thank them all. I think of my dear friend Ray, mentor Chuck, brother Joe, wife Alexandra, and a number of others who helped show me that hard work and determination were indeed a good thing. Be relentless in your passion and steadfast in your drive, and you will achieve all that is possible.

In the pursuit of any career, one needs the proper guidance and support. This idea, along with the ability to recognize the help offered in order to succeed, were constant thoughts in my mind. I was taught about the three Ds, all of which have served as daily reminders to stay on the road of my chosen path. Drive, determination, and devotion have served me well. I have kept these principals in the forefront of my being all these years. Unyielding determination *always* rose to the top of my daily thoughts and routine. I was fortunate during the early days to recognize these essential elements, and with steps, albeit baby ones, I slowly turned each step traveled into feet, yards, and later miles.

Journal Entry: November 17, 2004

The past few months seem to have passed in one brief minute. Where has the time gone? I have so much to write—where to begin? Since the start of the new symphony season, along with my personnel managing duties, I have also been playing in the percussion section every week. This particular week happens to be the first week off from playing in nearly two months. Because I am not playing, I find myself with a good deal of extra time on my hands. I usually had a good deal of free time during all rehearsals and performances, and so I brought my laptop with me each day so that I could begin catching up on all those loose ends I had been avoiding for the past few months. I had the best intentions of getting my work done, but every time I powered up my trusty ThinkPad, my first instinct was to go directly to my personal files, where I'd get lost updating my journal.

A few months ago, I decided I wanted to begin organizing my stories in a more concise way, but how? I started by printing the enormous file, over seven hundred pages. Once printed, the pile of loose-leaf measured nearly three inches of single-spaced, double-sided sheets. *What the heck do I do now?* I sat in silence staring at the pile of papers, contemplating my next move. Then it came to me. I started by breaking the journal down by year, then monthly in sequential order, and finally by categories. The categories outweighed the years and months combined. It seems I had a lot to say over the years.

In order to categorize the stories, I needed to scan the first few lines of each page to see what the particular topic was for that entry. There were stories of percussion lessons, foreign travel mishaps and memories, stories of lost instruments at the airports, and found happiness in the Czech Republic. Making movies, making friends, working with the famous and the not-so-famous, tears of pain, tears of joy and fears, thrills, apprehension, and aching muscles—the piles were growing and beginning to take form.

I may be crazy, but to keep these notes just for keepsake would be a sin.

With that in mind, I set a new goal for myself: sift through the entire journal, pick out some of the more interesting stories, and give them a major rewrite for later use.

Although most nights after work I am exhausted, I find myself committed to keeping good notes on daily or weekly events. I find myself with more notes and stories, more editing, more sifting, more to share. Drive, determination, and devotion once again take center stage in my life and newfound career.

I have been encouraged by so many to prepare these stories, and I am actually going to make my move. Who knows what will come of it? Perhaps this manuscript will remain a personal goal, and my stories will go unread by most. In the meantime, I find the sifting and reminiscing process cathartic and relaxing.

CONTENTS

CHAPTER 1

The Interview

The following interview took place while I was a professor at New Jersey City University.

December 19, 1999
Your full name: *James Albert Joseph Neglia*

Where you are from; background: *Enna, Sicily. I am a first-generation Italian American.*

Who inspired you to become a musician? *I would say my father, or moreover, my bloodline.*

Who inspires you today? *Not who, but what: my desire to entertain people and make a contribution to the musical world.*

What made you want to be a professional musician? *I remember hearing music from the radio through the speakers back in the early seventies. I wanted to live inside the speakers and do what I was hearing.*

Why percussion? *My first instrument was the piano, then violin, then trombone. Finally in 1976, my dad purchased a practice pad and some sticks. I was hooked. Nowadays, I like to drive the music through rhythmical pulse.*

Was there ever another career choice you had in mind? *I will be honest: no. I never thought about doing anything else but playing music my entire life. Even when my friends were going to school for music and taking another* double-major subject, I never got into it. They always said, "It is something to fall back on if music doesn't work." I always thought, "No way, not me!"

What made you want to teach music? *Teaching is an extension of playing. I am able to share with younger people my ideas and approach on performance. This is a great joy of mine.*

Why not just play? *Because I enjoy helping others. I feel the need to express my thoughts for anyone who desires to take the offerings.*

What are some of the joys and downfalls of teaching? *There are only a few disappointments to top the list. It really is depressing when I cannot connect with a student. Second, when a student really doesn't put his heart and soul into what he is doing, then I feel stifled and cannot help him.*

The joy is easy: connection, understanding, helping, sharing, enjoying, and learning.

What are some of the joys and downfalls of playing? *This is extremely difficult to answer. When I am really immersed, really into it, I can and have and will continue to enjoy a state of total and utter euphoria. It is almost like a heroin addict getting a dose of smack. I am elevated to a level that parallels none. That is why I stay in music. There is no other career that compares to it. In music there are not just momentary highs, but hours of highs. If a businessman closes a million-dollar deal, it is great for a while. However, if I perform Mahler, the feeling of satisfaction can last for days.*

The downside of being a performer is easy: I would say politics. The game of music can be a real drag—knowing who to know and what to say and when to say it. This is a topic for a dissertation!

What do you like the best about it? *Another good question: I like all of the above, but I also like the "hang," chatting with my colleagues, being part of a close-knit fraternity, the camaraderie and personal connection.*

What do you like the least about it? *Again, all of the above. We as full-time musicians live a 24-hour, 7–days-a-week, 365-days-a-year job. There is never a day off. Even if we are not working publicly, we are nearly always consumed with the art. It is like seeing a wonderful painting with all its colors and contrast; we are absorbed into the painting. The painting becomes part of* *us for a short period of time. With music, we are absorbed (and self-absorbed) every waking and non-waking moment of our lives.*

How does your career impact the rest of your life? *Oh man … here we go. Being a musician is very demanding, and some of the time—well, most of the time … no, all of the time—it requires sacrifice that tends to suck. I have missed more family functions, weddings, parties, Christmas events, ball games with the nieces and nephews, and more than I care to mention. The trick here is balance, just like in anyone else's life. Balance is the key. Just the right amount of red meat, drinks, cigarettes, and socializing will do the trick.*

What is a day in the life of Jim Neglia like? *Lora, I will write a book one day on this topic, really. But in short, a typical day might be: wake up, have coffee, turn the computer on, check e-mail. Then I hit the instruments for a while. Depending on the day, week, or month, I start by listening to music I need to learn. I often practice without hitting a single instrument; sometimes mental work is the best, and I can do it in the car while driving from gig to gig. After practicing, I will pack up whatever instruments I need for the afternoon rehearsal. Then I go to work, though I have never "worked" a day in my life. After rehearsal I generally have a late lunch or early dinner. I run home for my tuxedo and go to concert. When I get home I smoke a half dozen cigarettes, drink wine, check e-mail again, and pass out. The next day, I do it all over again with no complaints.*

If you could do it all over again, would you change anything? *No … but if I were to have just one, perhaps I would have higher goals.*

What would you say to aspiring musicians? *Think about commitment, goals, and balance, and practice your ass off. There are a thousand other people waiting for me to screw up and take my jobs.*

And last of all, in a world where too many people never find what it is they're looking for, especially in the career field, do you believe that you have found a career that is not just a job but a way of life? *Jesus, what a question! I have indeed found what I am looking for, but all the baggage that came with it, I could do without.*

One that you can honestly say you love? *Yes, indeed, I truly love my life, art, blessings, and life I chose.*

Do you have any additional comments? *These events helped shape my life into what it is today. I have been through a lot of anguish, both in my personal life and performance life. I have also shared happy tears, tears that have refocused my life. I have met a million people who have touched me in many ways. I have taken the good of all and wrapped myself around it. I have opened my life to certain sensitivities that most people are totally unaware even exist. For that I am sorry; people are missing out on bigger and better things of life. I have absolutely no power over anyone, just me and the direction I have chosen. I have written many pages in my computer, a kind of … diary—documenting certain gigs, people, places and events. It is a very interesting read. One day, I will have it published … First I need to write many more pages.*

The Article: A Professional Musician

Most people think a professional musician has an easy life—like that of a rock star. However, if we look at a working musician, one that makes their entire living playing music, we notice the hard work needed to make it in the industry. To be successful, one must have the commitment to practice and the will to constantly want to be better at what they do. It is a way of life, not a job.

Jim Neglia is not a rock star. He is a professional percussionist. His studies with Christopher Lamb (New York Philharmonic) at Mannes College of Music in New York have earned him a bachelor's in music and a master's in music. Jim is a man dedicated to playing and learning all that he can about music. Inspired by a desire to, in his words, "entertain people and make a contribution to musical statements," Jim is forever involved with music. He never has a "day off" from being a musician. If he is not performing, he is preparing mentally for the next gig, whether it is a lesson with a student or another show. This type of preparation is as important as it is to actually be sitting behind an instrument and playing. He might run down the pieces in his head, go through what he will teach in a lesson, or go over difficult sections in the piece he is about to perform. It is also a chance for him to clear out his mind so that he can concentrate on the gig he is on his way to. Jim is always consumed by his passion for music.

"I never thought about doing anything but playing music my entire life. I play daily, and not just in rehearsals but for personal entertainment and more importantly, fulfillment." To reach these levels of success, he stresses "commitment, goals, balance, and practice, practice, practice!" It takes *discipline*. The industry is highly competitive and political. If you do not work to be the best, you won't get the job. He adds, "There are 1000 other people waiting for me to mess up and take my job."

There may be many positions asking for a percussionist, but only one guy will get the salary. If he cannot do the job, he can easily be replaced.

Beginning in 1989 as Principal Timpanist for The New Philharmonic of New Jersey, Mr. Neglia performed professionally. As well as working in New Jersey, he commutes regularly to the Westchester Symphony Orchestra, the Harrisburg Symphony, and the National Grand Opera of New York. In 1996, Mr. Neglia was invited to be the primary Timpanist for the Prague Radio Symphony/Summer Festival in the Czech Republic. In 1997, the Szentendre Chamber Orchestra/Summer Festival in Hungary asked Jim to join their troupe. As well as orchestral work, Jim Neglia has played with classical performers, television personalities, and rock groups alike—Andrea Bocelli, Mel Tormé, Joan Rivers, Placido Domingo, and rockers The Moody Blues, and others. Also on his list of credits are performances and appearances in motion pictures such as *I Love NY*, with Christopher Plummer and Scott Biao and in *Joe Gould's Secret* with Stanley Tucci.

As a teacher at New Jersey City University, Mr. Neglia says that there are two downfalls: one, the depression when he cannot connect with a student, and two, when students don't really put their heart into what they are doing. For Jim, playing music is a "state of total and utter euphoria that elevates me to a level that parallels none." If he cannot make a person feel the passion and pure emotion that playing music makes him feel, Jim does not believe they experience all that music is and offers. For him it engulfs "every waking and non-waking moment of our lives." For Jim, music is life; like we need oxygen, Jim needs music.

Jim Neglia is one of the most genuine men anyone can meet. He has made his path exactly the way he wants it, and he has found joy in doing so. He has recognized what his passions are and made his life in them.

He says, "The trick is balance… just the right amount of red meat, drinks, cigarettes, and socializing will do it." Being a musician for Jim is not a career or a job, it is a lifestyle. And he genuinely loves every minute of it.

CHAPTER 2

Saturdays

In the early seventies, there was a radio broadcast show on WNYC called "Adventures in Good Music," with Karl Haas. I remember his lessons, musical descriptions, and explanations of works as well as his smooth and silky voice. The broadcast took place on Saturday mornings at 10:00 a.m. During this time, there was nothing more I wanted to do than to play outside with my friends, kicking the soccer ball, playing catch, or enjoying climbing the oddly-shaped tree in the side yard. However, my father had other ideas for my Saturday morning from ten to eleven. I was introduced to the Karl Haas show when I was just seven years old, and I remember sitting with my father from week to week, listening. He enjoyed the show thoroughly and would add more explanation for me on the heels of Haas's remarks. During the musical selections, he would explain in more depth what we were hearing. Karl Haas had much to offer, but my father had more.

My father, a musician himself, possessed talents in voice, piano, and composition. Although he was extremely dedicated to music, he needed to augment his living in order to help support his wife and five children. One way of making a considerable amount of extra income was to offer private piano lessons. It is my memory that, by 1968–69, he had amassed roughly forty half-hour lessons per week; all this while spending hours composing and holding a full-time job at the pharmaceutical company Hoffmann-La Roche. At some point, Dad made the decision to use the broadcast time to his advantage and cram in two more thirty-minute lessons. I couldn't blame him for doing it, but without him holding my hand, so to speak, my interest in the show dwindled rapidly. I am sure that he recognized in me the desire to hear, to learn, and to speak the language of music; after all, I showed sincere and strong interest when we listened together. I also believe that he had high hopes that one day I would make my living performing the great works we shared each weekend.

Dad came up with an idea that would enable him to hear his favorite program during his new working hours. His plan was for me to tape the program so that he could listen to it at a later time. He taught me how to operate the reel-to-reel tape deck, and I quickly learned how to swap out one reel for the next as quickly and smoothly as possible, missing the least possible amount of material with each change. The plan was simple and in theory should have worked without issue. What my father didn't know was that I would usually start the tape rolling and then go outside to play with my friends. I had no one supervising me except the tape deck, which ran independently. While outside enjoying my time, I would always keep an eye on my ever-trusty Timex, and when thirty minutes was approaching, I would dash inside to make the swap. At the appropriate time, I would click off the "record" switch, fast forward the reel to release the remainder of the first reel, and then thread the second reel through the fitted slot. When it was in place, I would hit "record," and after a second or two the reel would catch and pull the excess tape through the second reel to catch under the newly accumulating roll. Over the weeks, I became a master at switching the reels. I continued this pattern week after week, knowing that I had beaten the system. The best part was, my father was none the wiser—or so I thought.

Several weeks had passed when, much to my surprise, he asked me about a particular segment on the most recent broadcast. As I stood there with a blank expression on my face, unable to answer or even make something up, he knew that I had beaten his system. He knew that I had come up with some plan to avoid sitting through the hour, which had become torturous Saturday-morning pain. Without skipping a beat, he directed me to edit all commercials during the show. For the next year or so, I would sit listening to the show with my right hand on the pause switch, waiting for the commercial to come. By now I hated Karl Haas and that hour he stole from me each Saturday of my eighth year. When Haas's voice would begin to taper off, I knew we were seconds away from a station break. As the commercial would come on, I would turn the pause switch to the right, stopping the tape from further recording. For the next two agonizing minutes, I would listen to commercials on all topics ranging from public radio announcements to the Ford Motor Company announcing its new car. Like clockwork, two minutes later, the pause button would be released back to the left, and I recorded more Haas.

At the age of thirteen, I purchased my first drum set: a used, four-piece set of old Japanese, no-name brand drums that cost me a whopping thirty-five dollars of my hard-earned savings. I found the drums in a publication named the *Want Ad Press*, which was the precursor to eBay. The drums cleaned up nicely, and soon, after more yards and attics were cleaned and other chores completed, I added a few Camber cymbals to my setup. Within a few months, I was able to play along with my drumming idols on vinyl. My practice habits were beginning to take form.

By the time I was sixteen, I had developed strong feelings on the topic of work. I didn't want to *work*–I wanted to do with my life that which feels natural, so that I wouldn't have the sense of working. I always thought that *that* was the real key to success: to love your profession and never feel as though I was working. It wasn't until later in life that this idea assumed such a profundity. I cannot believe I had the foresight to even dream that thought back then.

By my senior year in high school, the time had come to think about higher education, but I never had the feeling that college was for me. "I am just not cut out for school," I remarked.

My mother responded, "No problem; you just need to go out and find a job—a *full-time* job." I couldn't imagine being in school, but what I *really* couldn't imagine was working for a living at some meaningless job just to make money. What a quandary!

I began thinking seriously about going to school for drummers—you know, to be a rock star or something like that. But the voice of reason, my mother, suggested that I learn *all* the instruments in the percussion family: the timpani, xylophone, marimba, and snare drum, as well as

9

the classical concert instruments, among them the triangle, tambourine, cymbals, bass drum, castanets, and more. This seemed to be the direction in which I was leaning and, ultimately I took her advice. Once agreed, I needed to find a teacher who was proficient in playing and teaching all those instruments.

I was a neophyte in percussion studies, and I believed that I could not possibly be accepted in any of the New York Conservatories. I began to research colleges within driving distance of our New Jersey home. We had little money to spend on schooling, and moving away was not an option. It had to be something local and not too expensive. During my research, I learned of a man named Tom Lester, a professor of percussion at William Paterson College (now William Paterson University). Because this was a state college, the tuition was affordable, and the short fifteen-mile ride was more than acceptable. This felt right to me, and I knew that I had to give it my best shot. I called the admissions office and inquired about what was required of me in order to be considered a freshman in the music department. A few days later, a complete package arrived with a full explanation of all requirements for undergraduates, along with endless forms and paperwork to be submitted.

In order to be accepted into the music program, I needed to take an audition in order to demonstrate to the adjudicator my basic skills and versatility on the snare drum, timpani, and any keyboard percussion instrument such as the marimba, vibraphone, or xylophone. This was a problem, because up to that time I had formally studied only the drum set (with Master Carl Wolfe). Although I had played some church gigs on the timpani, I really wasn't prepared to demonstrate anything more than the absolute basics. But then, after learning Lester was not available for private lessons, I had to do additional research, one result of which was that I learned that one of the professors who then taught percussion at William Paterson lived just fifteen minutes from my home. I called him, introduced myself, and explained my situation. It was then that I learned that the audition was just six weeks away! My next question to him was. "When can we start?"

Ted Stern agreed to help prepare me for the upcoming audition. Together we organized an appropriate selection of snare-drum scores as well as a short marimba work and a timpani etude. For the next five and a half weeks, I was a cave-dweller in my basement, not allowing myself to come upstairs until I was sure that my practicing had reached a higher level than the one at which I began the session. There were frustrations. Week after week, Ted drove me harder and harder, telling me, "It isn't good enough to get in yet. Work harder!" I worked diligently with a metronome and mirror. The metronome helped keep me squarely in time, and the mirror forced me to see if my stick and hand positions were identical, left matching right. I spent hours and hours each day preparing my selections for the audition, never thinking about abandoning my primary goal: get into college and avoid working for a living. My hands began forming themselves around the sticks, becoming one with the piece of wood I held for so many hours each day. I remember feeling as though I had never wanted anything so badly in my life. *I want it, I am going to get it, and no one can stop me.* At night, when I was lying in bed waiting to fall asleep, I would air practice my exercises and etudes, in order to discover how much I had committed to memory. I could hear the snap of the drum in my ears, as if I was actually hitting the instrument. I began to feel it. *I believe that I am ready.*

Audition day. After parking my car and grabbing my mallets from the front seat, I made my way to the cement stairwell on the north side of the building, which leads to the lower level of Shea Auditorium, home of the music department. Once in the building, I found myself standing almost in front of room 108, the percussion studio and location of my soon-to-be audition. As I stepped into the room, I was quickly overwhelmed by the sheer mass of the percussion equipment in this thirty feet by thirty feet percussion studio. There were marimbas, vibraphones, crotales, fifteen or more timpani, tubular bells, and even an upright piano. As I panned the room, it was hard not to notice the shelving that ran from floor to ceiling on the far wall. Every inch of the shelving was crammed with smaller accessories for the percussionists' needs. Graduated tom-toms, tambourines, woodblocks, sound effects, and cymbals of every size were placed meticulously on the shelves. There were multiple cymbals, and tom-tom and snare drum stands for at least a dozen drums. Sitting about seven feet above the tambourine shelf were roughly twenty snare drums of every make, material, and dimension. I felt like a kid lost in a candy shop.

It was time to refocus on the purpose for my trip: the audition. After checking the folded paper I had stuffed into my upper-left shirt pocket,

I confirmed room 108 was where I needed to be. I began to unpack my snare drum sticks, timpani, and marimba mallets, carefully placing them next to the preset instruments in the room. I began warming up on the only snare drum that was set up. I was tapping, rolling, and executing specific rudiments that I had been using for my warm-up routine for the past six weeks. During this routine, a man walked into the room. At first he didn't say a word; he was simply roaming about aimlessly. With no idea who he was or why he was there, I continued warming up. After completing the final rudiment, he asked me if I was ready. "Sure thing," I responded, "I am just waiting for the panel to arrive so I can begin."

The man chuckled as he introduced himself. "Hello, Jim. I am Tom Lester." I couldn't believe it! At first sight, I thought he was the janitor of the building! He was dressed in dull green pants with a matching shirt. With little more to say, I gulped once and motioned I was indeed ready to play for him.

I had prepared so thoroughly that I was not the slightest bit nervous about the actual audition. I just wanted to play for Tom and show him what I had prepared. A short fifteen minutes later, he informed me that I had been accepted into the music program, and would be starting in the fall. I had sailed through the seemingly easy torture session, unscathed by what should have unnerved anyone in my position. I headed home, my head miles in the sky, and shared the good news with my family. Later, I called my teacher as well.

That summer, after the audition, I began focusing on refining my playing, seriously honing in on as much as I possibly could. With every stroke of the stick, I knew more and more that I wanted to play music for my living. Further, I had a sense that I was gravitating toward the more serious repertory: classical music. Who wants to be a rock star? Well, I did, but my inner voice was telling me that it was a million-to-one shot, that I had a much better chance of winning an orchestra gig one day than becoming a famous rock star. With that realization, my determination took me to a new level. I began to really understand what was needed in order to excel in this field.

A few months after my triumph at the audition, a flyer was posted on the bulletin board at William Paterson announcing several openings in the New York Youth Symphony. Two openings were in the percussion section, and one was for the principal timpani position of this prestigious group. I remember reading the notice and thinking, *This sounds as though it would be a lot of fun—and right up my alley.* Having just won the William Paterson College audition a few months earlier, I thought I could pull together the material needed to audition for the Youth Symphony. What I didn't know (or think of) was that the other applicants auditioning for the vacancies would most likely be from the Manhattan School of Music, the Juilliard School, and the Mannes College of Music—not William Paterson College in New Jersey. Back to the basement I went, this time armed with tons of new materials and renewed determination.

I submitted my application and a few weeks later received an audition time and date for late August. I worked methodically on the required excerpts and solo selections I was to perform. I prepared just as I did for the William Paterson test many months earlier. On the appointed day, my brother-in-law drove me to Forty-eighth Street and Park Avenue. Here we go again. I don't remember being nervous or scared, just a bit anxious about the process. In addition to our display on keyboard percussion, timpani, and snare drum, we were required to demonstrate our general knowledge of hand-held percussion instruments: the triangle, tambourine, cymbals, and bass drum. We were allotted twenty minutes to show the adjudicators what we had to offer. The audition itself was a blur. When I opened my eyes again, it was over. I knew that I had played well and provided a good representation of my abilities, but I kept thinking, *Was it up to New York standards?*

As fate would have it, I won the principal timpani chair with the Orchestra. I was shocked and ecstatic, blown away and beside myself with joy, flooded with near disbelief. Now back to the basement to begin further preparations for the next chapter of my young musical life: Carnegie Hall.

A few short weeks later, I began college and also started rehearsals with the New York Youth Symphony. I was exhilarated, pumped, and focused beyond words. Along with my scholastic duties, I began working on the literature for my Carnegie Hall debut in November of 1981, which included the Brahms *Academic Festival Overture* and Robert Schumann's *Symphony No. 1*, the *Spring Symphony*. Never having heard these works before, I made my way to the listening lab in music department of Shea

Auditorium. Armed with my printed music, I went to give these works my first hearing. As I sat down on the hard wooden chair, fixing the oversized head phones around my ears, I kept thinking about how fortunate I was to have this remarkable opportunity to perform at Carnegie Hall. After loading the cassette tape into the dispenser, I hit the play button. Here comes the Academic Festival Overture. Much to my surprise, the melody sounded familiar; had I already heard the selection before? I continued listening, and midway through the overture, in the back of my mind I could hear Karl Haas talking about Brahms and this very famous overture. At that moment, I clutched my pencil, dropped my music to the floor, and closed my eyes tightly in disbelief. Old memories came flooding back as if through a shattered dam. Could it be, really? I never thought I would feel the need to thank Karl Haas for taking all those precious Saturday mornings away from me so long ago. Only after recognizing the overture did I fully understand how his show had helped shape my life and work to come.

Journal Entry: February 22, 1983

Much to my surprise, while performing "Night Music" by Jay Gatch, my brother Joe appeared in the audience. Why did he come to this performance? I couldn't imagine. The Gatch composed for a chamber group, utilizing a percussionist, alto saxophone, piano, violin, and a timpanist. My duties included a substantial xylophone part as well as multiple tom-toms, suspended cymbals, hand percussion, and a vibraphone part. I was surrounded by percussion instruments. I was thoroughly prepared and ready to go. I had worked harder than ever learning the part properly, paying clear attention to dynamics as well as working out all of the choreographed movements.

To my brother, it was obvious. At the conclusion of the performance, Joe came to congratulate me on a well-executed performance. He went on to inform me that it was time for me to move on—it was time for me to leave New Jersey and begin my studies in the big apple, New York City. He said this, and I began to feel my life change.

CHAPTER 3

College Days

*"The arts are not a way of making a living. They are a very human
way of making life more bearable. Practicing an art, no matter how
well or badly, is a way to make your soul grow, for heaven's sake.
Sing in the shower. Dance to the radio. Tell stories. Write a poem to
a friend, even a lousy poem. Do it as well as you possibly can. You
will get an enormous reward. You will have created something."*

—Kurt Vonnegut

I spent the better part of my college life locked away in a practice room
and standing over a snare drum, timpani, and marimba for hours. Most
days I spent an average of ten hours honing my skills. Some days I would
play so much that I didn't have the strength to leave school and find my
way home. I would wake up in the morning to find myself under an
instrument in a dark, cold studio at the Mannes College of Music in
New York City.

It was routine to fight the discomfort in my muscles from overuse; slowly
building endurance one muscle at a time was the ultimate challenge.
Swollen forearms, thumbs, and index fingers were unable to pinch
another second, and a weary mind was seemingly brainwashed by my
chosen discipline. I wanted to succeed so desperately, and at times I
found myself in deep physical, if not mental, trouble. Sometimes aspirin
would dull the pain; other times stronger medication was desired.

While winding down from a practice, there was always a moment when
my muscles and mind were in harmony and at peace, without thinking

15

of making music. Some would call it being in the zone. It was easier in these moments to accept the pain of learning, practicing, wanting, and needing—the relentless vibrations of every stroke penetrated my very being. It was also easier to accept that there was only a remote chance of winning a job as an orchestra musician. Like an appendage that cannot be removed without complete destruction, it is always better to feel our art fully than to think about surviving without it. This was my daily torture, one that I grew to love and respect, and one that caused me to push on through the mental and physical pain.

The nagging question I had was, how can we fully dedicate our lives to the arts with complete heart, mind, and soul, when the dark cloud of doubt is always hovering overhead? How will we live? Where will we work? These were hard questions I needed to answer. But the most difficult question that needed answering was, "How can I live, be, exist *without* music?"

It is understood that parents want what is best for their children. However, life in the arts does not rank in the top-ten professions to bestow upon young ones. Why would parents wish this most uncertain career on their children? My feeling was that most *didn't* want this. In reality, most of the people who went to school around the same time I did, who aspired to be full-time, working musicians, had the same family story: "You can go into music, but have a second major in mind, *just in case* the first one doesn't work out." In my case, I had a family who embraced my dreams of working in the arts. They supported and nurtured my dream, even making my life as easy as they could, to help ensure that I would succeed in my chosen path.

Journal Entry: March 23, 2003

Last night I went to Juilliard to hear my nephews in a performance. In the first half of the performance, during the stage change, I realized that 99 percent of these extremely talented kids would be jobless when they graduated. Unable to find work, many will experience real pain through their chosen course in the music world. I feel awful for each and every one of them. What will they do to survive?

Adding to my grueling daily workout was the alarm sounding at 5:00

a.m., then the commute into New York City and parking my car. Eleven courses each semester—including lessons, practicing, contemporary ensemble, orchestra rehearsal, percussion ensemble, chorus rehearsals, repertoire class, Western civilization, art history, and more—contributed to the hectic process. Along with my studies in school, I began performing as a young professional musician. I played small concerts in churches, student recitals, and with some semi-professional orchestras around New York and New Jersey.

Journal Entry: April 11, 1985

From the onset, school can be a tremendous struggle. Regardless of the school's location, in state or out, we are tossed into our new four-year home, where the struggle can be compounded by anything from a language barrier to sexual orientation. Regardless, one needs to adapt to their new climate quickly, and with as little fear as possible.

Beyond the physical location and people who surrounded me, at times I felt an internal struggle between love and hate, happiness and sorrow, needs and wants. I loved attending school but at times had difficulties with the commute. My needs are as basic as one can imagine; show up on time to classes, lessons and performing obligations. A good meal and the support of my family, teachers, and friends are all part of the scene as well, all needed, all cherished. Although I have an amazing support system, I never really found the balance between school, home life, and life itself. In spite of my head playing tricks on me, I somehow managed to come out in the end stronger and more focused than I ever imagined. My determination was never in question; neither would I allow any force inside or otherwise to interfere with my primary purpose. No matter the pain, nothing could ever diminish my love of music.

While attending college, I was fortunate to live at home. Although my folks had split up years earlier, never once in the course of schooling was I asked for a nickel to live under the roof provided by my family. They were more concerned about my studies, dedication, and travels to the city each day than they were about teaching me a lesson in paying rent. Yes, I was blessed, and I knew it.

Although I was spared of the burden of housing expenses, I was still responsible for all my own bills: car insurance, gas, round-trip bus tickets, subway tokens, books, mallets, instruments, music, and on occasion some decadent lunch from the Chinese restaurant up the block from school. To help save money, I would go to the public libraries and spend hours on end photocopying books and repertoire parts, paying no attention to the copyright laws. To save money on purchasing records, I would purchase blank cassettes so that I could tape musical selections off the radio and use them as study guides. Every penny saved built up to a dollar spent on instruments, music, mallets, or some other item I needed to help aid my career.

During my school years, I worked as hard as possible to make money. The summers would be the best time to make some real cash, because I had more time on my hands and the weather warranted it. I would mow and manicure my neighbor's lawns and clean attics. As fate would have it, in the fall of 1981 I followed in my family's footsteps and landed a job singing in a church. Both brothers and both sisters, along with my father, worked in various parishes throughout New Jersey. Now we all had our own church jobs, playing organ or singing for weddings, funerals, and weekend masses. The good old church came through for the Neglia family in a large way. I was the new leader of song at St. Joseph's Roman Catholic Church in Jersey City, where I received fifteen dollars per mass for my efforts. I earned an amazing sixty dollars for the four masses per week. My new gig at the church, some freelance work I had secured, and the work-study program at school assisted in helping me meet my financial obligations. The Mannes College of Music offered me the position of orchestra librarian at five dollars per hour. Things were looking up, and my trips to the corner Chinese restaurant began to increase ever so slightly.

With the acceptance of the Mannes job came more responsibility. I knew nothing about being an orchestral librarian or the duties involved, yet I accepted the job. I later learned that my duties included supplying musicians with music for upcoming concerts, filing old parts back into the vast library collection, keeping track of parts musicians had and from what string stand it came, and numbering string parts with the corresponding player so that I could confirm who returned music and who didn't. The hardest part of the job was placing bowings into actual parts; up bows and down bows had to be transferred from all principal players' parts into the section parts. The process of adding the bowings to each part took hours to complete. As much of a pain in the neck as it was, though, I was happy for the additional work. I accepted my new duties and studied up on how I could excel in the position, about which I knew so little. An added benefit from all this was that I was adding to my organizational skills, something that would serve me well later in life.

During my first semester in New York, my uncle had a stroke and died a week later. He passed the day before my nineteenth birthday, on October 23, 1983. Unc, as we affectionately called him, lived with us the last few years of his life, so our relationship was close. This magnified the pain I was feeling, and it was something I had never experienced before. In our typically-European family, when someone in our immediate family died, we all gathered at their bedside in the hospital to say our good-byes. Once we received the phone call that the end was near, we made our way to the hospital. My uncle passed fifteen minutes before I arrived; his body was still warm. I spent a few minutes reflecting on his life, and I held his hand one last time. This was our way of saying our private good-bye—no funeral home atmosphere, and no smell of flowers to permeate the room, just Uncle John and his family.

November rolled around, and school was in full force. I had been assigned to perform with the contemporary ensemble to play a selection of music by acclaimed composer George Crumb. I hoped this would be a good diversion from my misery; I felt it would help keep my mind off Unc's absence. I was excited about playing this particular concert, because we were told that Mr. Crumb himself would be in attendance. I had studied some of his music while attending William Paterson College, and I was particularly intrigued by his abilities to score music. Crumb used percussion instruments not just for punctuation and rhythm, but for coloring the mood of the music. The kalimba (a pitched thumb piano), Icelandic prayer stones, and blowing into a jug were all common practices in his rich yet subtle scoring.

Concurrently with my uncle dying, and my dedicating myself to the contemporary ensemble, my brother, whom I shared a bedroom with on the third floor of our home, decided it was time for us to separate. Our house was not equipped to offer us both a standard room, so I decided to claim the basement as my new area. My instruments were already filling the vast space, so bringing my bed to join the room seemed to be the next logical step. I spent the first few nights down in the cellar without incident. However by the end of my first week, I had experienced a horrible fright.

The basement of our house was below ground level, so when the lights were out, my room, which had no window in it, was as dark as molasses. I was in the habit of keeping a candle and book of matches close to my bed, in the event I needed to get up during the night. I had arrived home quite late from school and was extremely tired; I was beginning to feel the pressures of school, life, and work. I unpacked my bag of the day's events and repacked for the one yet to come. Unable to keep my eyes open any longer, I lit the candle and shut the main light off. I plopped my exhausted body onto the bed, and began to settle down. I was sure it would be no more than a few short minutes before I drifted into oblivion.

The room was unusually quiet—almost too quiet. I lifted my head off the pillow to blow out the candle. With the blackness of the night came an uncertainty that could not be explained. Within a few minutes, I sensed a presence in my room, a *strong* presence that was unmistakably there. What the heck was happening? Who was here? At first I blamed it on fatigue and my weary mind. But no, without a doubt someone was in my room with me. I could feel it beside me! I retraced my steps before getting into bed. I had performed my regular ritual of locking the doors leading to the basement, so there was no possible way to enter the room unnoticed. At this point my mind was racing. Was I dreaming? Definitely not. Could I be hallucinating? But if I thought I may be hallucinating, could I really be doing so? No. Who the heck was here with me? In absolute fear, I moved my right hand slowly toward the waiting book of matches. I felt the need to light the candle that lay inches away, to see for myself who had come to visit. As I picked up the matches, I could smell a very familiar smell. Was it really the scent of my uncle, who had died two weeks earlier? My heart began beating faster and faster. Fear and then calm embraced me. I began to talk out loud. "Unc, if this is you, then I am requesting you to please go away. I do not want to see you now." I was really genuinely terrified, for I was certain he was with me.

Next thing I knew, his smell was all over me, his presence all around me, and his heartbeat in my ears. My mouth went dry. I was afraid to strike the match because I knew if I did, I would surely see him in full form, for he *was* right next to me! Time seemed to have been at a standstill, and the silence was deafening. The whole episode lasted about half a minute at most, but it felt as if an hour was closing in. I realized this could not be happening to me—and if it *was* actually happening, then I should be happy to see my late uncle. I built up my nerve and courage to strike the match, fully expecting to see him standing in front of me. As the match ignited, my eyes adjusted to the newly shone light, and it became obvious that no one was in my room. No one was in the basement, and no one had entered the house.

To this day, I *know* my uncle was in my room with me that night. My uncle had lived with us for the last few years of his life, and he had suffered from Parkinson's. I never knew how to deal with his condition, and therefore I was rarely around to help him when he was in need. When he died, I felt guilty for almost never helping and not expressing my love for him the way I knew I could. Perhaps he came to offer me his understanding of my weakness, his unconditional love. I do believe that was the true intention for his visit. It was not to scare me, but to help me along with my feelings of despair.

A few weeks later, Thanksgiving was approaching, which meant final exams were not far off. On the Friday before Thanksgiving, I arrived at school at my normal time and began my normal routine, which was to practice. By the time the clock struck 7:00 a.m., I had put in a solid hour on the vibraphone; phrasings and pedaling were my focus. I was unable to continue to play because my head was killing me, and I was dripping with sweat. Although the temperature in the building was a comfortable seventy degrees, I was freezing. On Fridays I had only one class, music theory, which ran from nine to ten. At about seven, I stepped outside the percussion room for a drink of juice. I dropped fifty cents into the vending machine, pressed the orange juice button, and began to sip the cool drink slowly. I sat on the only seat in the room, a large, black, furry couch that was more comfortable than my own bed at home. I put my head back on the soft cushion, and in less than a minute I was out cold.

At about 10:15 I felt someone put a hand on my shoulder. My theory teacher woke me from a very deep sleep. She was a mother herself, took one look at me, and suggested I go home. My complexion was ashen and my forehead felt hot. I was barely able to pick myself up from the couch. Once in the car, I crossed from the East Side to the West via Seventy-ninth Street. After turning left onto Tenth Avenue, I headed south for the Lincoln Tunnel. I miraculously made it home within thirty minutes.

Once home, bed seemed like the logical place to be. I plopped my exhausted body onto my bed and pulled the thick, warm quilt over my shivering body. Evening had rolled around when Mom returned from work. She entered my room and was surprised to see me sleeping at such an early hour. After feeling my head with her lips, she yelled for my brother's assistance. I remember that they picked up my limp body, undressed me, and put me under the cutting coldness of the showerhead. Minutes later an ambulance arrived and transported me to St. Michaels Medical Center in Newark. My temperature had reached a life-threatening 104.7 degrees.

By the time we reached the medical center, I was incoherent and nearly comatose. This arrival would be the last thing I remembered for several days to come. The doctors began their mission to diagnose me. They performed a CAT scan, which turned out negative. Following the CAT scan was a spinal tap. I was told that a spinal tap is an extremely painful test, but I would not know, because I felt nothing and have no memory of the whole incident. Thanksgiving came and went—what did I care, I was still unsure I was alive. I had slipped into a comatose state for more than five days. My family had feared the worst, and the doctors gave them no reassurance. After ruling out viral and spiral meningitis, drug abuse, and a list of other ailments, the doctors were perplexed.

A few days after the holidays, I woke up in an unfamiliar room. Where was I? Better yet, why was I here, wherever here was? A week of my life was lost, and I was none the wiser. The final diagnosis was that I had suffered from cluster headaches brought on by stress, excess coffee drinking, and too much smoking. The blood vessels in my brain constricted and would not release, thus causing a chain reaction of repercussions internally. After five days, the blood vessels in my brain began to relax, and I was offered a second chance, which I would never forget or ignore.

While recovering, I remember questioning myself. *Why should I continue going to school, if I am only going to end up here every time the stress reaches this level? Why put myself through this nightmare?* As the days passed, I began to recover physically, but mentally I was going nowhere. *What now? Depression? No way.* Family and friends began to visit regularly, and my physical state started to improve rapidly. One day while on the road to recovery, my mother asked me if there was anything I wanted her to bring to me from home. The only thing I could think of was my Walkman and a stack of classical cassettes from my room. Beethoven, Brahms, and even Bartok assisted in my recovery that fateful November. Although stuck in the hospital for several more days, the music helped me dramatically in the recovery process. While listening, I was reminded of how art was a part of my inner fabric, and with that, my mental recovery began to take hold. It was during a listening of the second movement of Beethoven's *Symphony No. 7* that I realized I needed to be in it, and for the long haul. After that I never looked back, not even for one minute.

CHAPTER 4

I Love NY

Journal Entry: September 28, 1986

A telephone call came through the switchboard at the Mannes College of Music from the Central Casting Company. The company sought a drummer to perform in a motion picture, to be released later that year. As fate would have it, I was in the office at the right time. In addition, I was the only student percussionist in the school who had his own drum set and a car to transport them.

After discussing the terms with the casting agency, I took the gig. I was to bring a set of drums to the corner of Seventy-second Street and Central Park West, set up, and perform as a street musician. Sounds easy enough; why not? My call was for 5:30 a.m. three days later. I needed to arrive on time so I could sign in, go to wardrobe, and be ready to set up my drums in a flash. The night before the filming, I meticulously packed my drum kit. I double-checked and then triple-checked that every part of the kit was securely packed in its case, and then I stored them in my car overnight for an easy, early-morning departure. I could not sleep at all because I was hyped up and nervous. I couldn't think of what rhythms to play when directed. Maybe a samba or funk beat, or a rock beat. I ran the patterns through my head until at some point exhaustion set in, and I fell into a deep sleep.

The alarm rang, and with one quick movement I jumped out of bed and hit the off button. I ran to the shower and was in and out in three minutes flat. I grabbed my jeans, put on a shirt, picked up my camera, and ran to the car. I sat in the driver's seat and noticed that a total of six minutes had passed from the time the alarm had rung to this moment. Suddenly I remembered to look in the back of my car. Were my drums here? Did I leave the house without them? The kit was right where I'd left it the night before: on the back, folded-down seat of my 1978 Volkswagen Rabbit. I turned the key, and off I went. In just three miles, I was taking the on-ramp to enter Route 3 east, which took me to the Lincoln Tunnel. No traffic whatsoever. Through the tunnel and left onto Fortieth Street. I proceeded uptown on Tenth Avenue and then cross-town on Sixty-second Street to avoid the heavy morning rush. Still no traffic. I could not recall the last time I drove into the city without the hassle of weaving in and out of traffic. Was I in a time warp? I made a left onto Central Park West and then went uptown a few more few blocks until I had obviously reached the right stop. Trailers lined Seventy-second Street—but there were no people in sight.

I pulled up to the first trailer, kissed its bumper, and turned off my ignition. Where was everyone? I looked at my watch. Hands showing 4:10 a.m. stared me in the face! My excitement had taken over the entire event. I remember setting the alarm for 3:30, but how did I wake, shower, drive, and arrive in forty minutes? I guess this was the true definition of an adrenaline rush.

The pay for all this angst would be the princely sum of $150, though for me it was not about the paycheck; the money was not even an issue. As I sat on a park bench, waiting for the sun to rise, I began to think about the day to come. The stars of the movie, *I Love NY*, included Scott Baio and Christopher Plummer. How exciting all of this was for me! I was twenty-two years old and making a movie in New York City!

As the morning progressed, tables of food and drink were placed strategically throughout the area. Fruits, cheeses and half a dozen types of bread sat on the tables, just waiting for consumption. Coffee and tea waited in thermoses, piping hot, with three types of sugar and four kinds of milk. What an amazing display, all for me! That was truly the way I felt. In fact, the most remarkable aspect of the whole gig would turn out to be the amount of time I spent sipping coffee and sitting around, waiting to be called for my scene.

Minutes ticked by and slowly turning into hours … several hours. Finally my time came. It was 3:00 p.m.—I had been waiting around for nearly eleven hours. I erected my drum kit in record time, sat on my throne, and awaited further instruction. The director came over and asked me to play for him. "What would you like to hear?" I asked.

He replied, "How about 'Take Five'?" It was a popular Dave Brubeck tune. "No problem. Let's do it."

I began my 5/4 groove, carefully executing the fifth beat. I eventually looked up to see the director's reaction; a grin on his face from ear to ear. "Perfect!" he shouted.

The scene would be simple: I play, they film, and it's over. Right? Wrong! The real scene would be this: I set up my kit on the corner of Seventy-second Street and Central Park West and begin playing. A motorcycle speeds into view, heading east on Seventy-second Street. It skids to a halt next to my kit, followed by a car chasing the lone biker. In addition, there are to be four kids riding skate boards, heading north on Central Park West. All these actions need to be timed out perfectly in order for the scene to look real. At the time the motorcycle is to skid by my kit, the kids should be within striking distance to pull off the illusion that the skid was really too close to all of us. If shot from the south side of Seventy-second Street with the angle facing uptown, the illusion should work perfectly.

The crew set the scene. The director shouted, "Action!" through a bull horn, and the cameras started rolling.

> **Take 1:** The motorcycle missed its mark. "Cut!" rang out across the set.

> **Take 2:** The skid was perfect; but imperfectly, I failed to react. Nobody told me I was supposed to react. I was there merely to play my kit, no? The director approached and asked if I was nervous about the motorcycle's proximity to my seat. I replied, "Yes." He followed up with, "Well, then, *react* to the fear!" I nodded my head up and down and apologized for not knowing better.

Take 3: You know the old saying, "The third time's a charm"? Well, the third time was like nothing I had ever expected. They called for silence, the director yelled, "Action!" and I began to play, settling into a groove immediately. Out of the corner of my eye, I could see the motorcycle coming. It was gaining speed, and I surely did not think he was going to be able to slow down, let alone stop before he would hit me. At that moment, no acting lessons were necessary when the bike skidded to within two feet of my drums. I toppled off my throne to the pavement below, shaking and in a panic. *Christ! I am going to die on West Seventy-second Street!* The skateboards went flying, and the car chase followed through their mark and finished perfectly. My heart was racing as I heard the director yell, "Cut! It's a print!" I had no idea what was going on. What was a print? What had happened? Was it okay, was I still alive? Why was everyone clapping? A couple of the workers slapped me on the back. "That's all; you can pack up and go home."

My day was suddenly over, and I realized how exhausted I really was—and I still needed to pack up! I stowed my gear back into my Rabbit in reverse order of how I took it out. As I was packing up, a guy came up to me and asked to see my SAG card. "What's an SAG card?" was my response.

"Screen Actors Guild employment card," he shot back.

"I don't have one; I'm just a student who grabbed a day's work."

Although I had already packed my cymbals, the drums were still set up, The guy pulled a tape measure from his jacket pocket. *What the heck is he doing?* I thought as he measured the distance from the skid marks to my drum set. He turned to me and asked if I would sign a few papers. I hesitantly signed everything he offered and went on my way, not knowing what had just happened.

About a month passed before an envelope from the Casting Company arrived. I opened it to find not only the originally agreed-to amount of $150, but also a check in the amount of $1,486.57! In shock I shouted to my brother, who was standing right beside me, "Look at this, look what

I got!" The statement accompanying the check explained: $150 flat pay, breakfast break, lunch break, dinner break, overtime, and a category I'd never heard of: "still time." However, the bulk of the check was for my performance as "stuntman." Yes, a stuntman! The whole episode with the tape measure replayed in my head. Obviously the proximity of the skid marks to my drum kit had put me in harm's way. Move over, Jackie Chan!

I Love NY was released nine months later in movie theaters for all to see. After watching the movie, I stayed in the nearly-empty theater for the credits to be displayed. There I was, listed in two separate places. The first simply said "street musician," and the second was much more impressive, "stuntman."

CHAPTER 5

Hearts

Journal Entry: February 14, 1986

It was Valentine's Day, and my girlfriend had given me a small Valentine's Day gift. Her little care package included a beautiful card, along with a long-stemmed rose and a small box of hearts. These are the candy hearts with little sayings on them, like "Love you," "Miss you," and "Be mine." I tucked them into my tuxedo pocket and departed for my day's work in Queens.

I headed out on Route 3 east to the Lincoln Tunnel, cross-town to the Queens Midtown Tunnel, and finally up the LIE. I arrived at Queens College without incident and began to unpack my instruments. I found the music on this particular concert to be challenging. Because most of the works required rock-steady tempo, accuracy, and a very steady hand, I had abandoned all caffeine from my diet three weeks prior. In addition, I had been working on breathing exercises to help keep me calm; I would use these techniques when I felt I needed them most. The exercises seemed to help.

The concert began with the "Symphonic Suite" to *Porgy and Bess*. In this work, the principal percussionist is called upon to play a very difficult, tricky, *loud* xylophone part. The part is something we spend hours, months, and even years in the practice room shedding. The part is a flurry of sixteenth notes performed in rapid succession with accents interspersed throughout each passage, moving from right hand to left and then back again. I was going to perform this work for the first time in my career—nerve-wracking.

Following the Gershwin was Hanson's *Symphony No. 2*, titled "The Romantic." There were both cymbals as well as snare drum in this work. I chose to play the snare drum part. Filled with smooth rolls, I was able to use this selection as a warm-up for what was to come after intermission.

The second half of the show began with *The Stiegmeister Clarinet Concerto*. I decided to take this work off in preparation of the finale of the day. This proved to be a rather large mistake. As I sat in the green room fidgeting, I felt the small article in my pocket. The box of Valentine's Day hearts I had received just a few hours ago was calling my name. I cracked the box open and began to consume them, one by one, reading the messages before popping them into my mouth. It wasn't until there were just a few remaining at the bottom of the box that I realized that these little sweets were one hundred percent sugar cubes. Having been off caffeine and sugar for nearly a month, I was really fearful of how my body would react to the candy. I am only sorry that one of these hearts didn't say "Sugar, dummy!" It was too late; what was done was done, and there was no reversing it. I tried to stay focused on the music at hand, but I kept thinking about my absolute stupidity in eating those little treats.

At the start of the second half, the principal clarinetist took his place center stage, in solo position. It wasn't until that moment that I realized in about thirty minutes I would be standing in the same position. The concerto was well received by the audience, and now it was my turn. Just after the applause died down, I watched as the stagehands carefully placed my snare drum in its proper position. While this was happening, our music director, Jenna, recounted a recent concert that had aired just nights before our live performance. It was a broadcast of The New York Philharmonic with Zubin Mehta conducting the same selection as our finale, Ravel's *Bolero*. She asked me if I had seen the broadcast. "Yes," I responded, "and furthermore, my teacher was playing the snare drum part."

She followed up with, "Did you see Mehta? He was dripping wet during the performance. *Bolero* is a nothing piece to conduct, just bring in each player and guide them along their individual solos, right?"

I looked at her and had no real response. Then I told her, "Okay, let me get out there and prepare for the *Bolero*."

She looked at me insistently and said, "No, I want you to enter with me, the same as any other soloist would do."

Gulp, was my first reaction, "Fine," was my second. A few moments later, off we went.

The audience responded with applause as we both took our places. Once set, our eyes met; I nodded in acknowledgment. I was ready. I never thought about the sugar hearts, not for a moment. I am convinced that all the mental preparation I had done was anchoring me to the stage and drum set before me. On the flip side, I was terrified because of my new stage placement. We'd had no sound check with me in that position. Jenna's spontaneity of having me up front was incredibly stressful. I felt unsure about my starting dynamic. I knew I would need to play even softer up front than I would if I were in my normal position, in the back of the orchestra. All this was going through my head while I calmly looked down to make sure my sticks were in position. They were. I noticed that my shirt was moving; it was my heart pounding.

As she lifted her hands, preparing with the upbeat, I lifted my sticks, over the very edge of my ever-reliable Hinger touch-tone snare drum. Her hands were about to come down when she stopped mid-motion. There were people in the audience coughing, and coughing, and coughing. She waited for only a few seconds, but it felt like so much longer; time stood still.

Once again she lifted her hands, and this time the audience was so quiet one could hear a pin drop. Then off we went. The opening four measures are complete solo measures for the snare drum, only to be accompanied by pizzicato in the celli. Much to my amazement, I could barely hear myself play. Was it too soft? Or was I just lost in the blind white noise with which I have become so familiar? Jenna glanced over at me and smiled a smile that put me completely at ease. I knew I was in the pocket, both dynamically and with her tempo.

Somewhere in the fifth or sixth minute of this exercise in dynamic control, I had the guts to look up. I wasn't using any music, so why should

I look up? Because I wanted to enjoy the moment as much as I possibly could. I needed to connect with the audience, and all around me. As I lifted my head, I saw hundreds of eyes staring at me, or what I perceived as staring. It didn't really matter at the time, because I knew that I was the center of focus. As I panned the audience from right to left, Jenna came into my vision. I have always found her to be a remarkably beautiful woman, and with an added attraction: she is from Italian descent. Maybe I found her incredibly sexy because of her musical gifts; perhaps it was due to her absolute certainty while conducting the orchestra. Maybe all of these things were true, but when our eyes met, I saw the loveliest vision one could place their eyes on in a lifetime. Jenna was dripping from perspiration, conducting this work in a completely seductive way. It was obvious that she was enjoying every moment as much as I was. Our eyes locked for just a few seconds, and then she refocused on the music around her. During the next few minutes, I recall thinking about our pre-*Bolero* conversation regarding Mehta. I was grinning from ear to ear and living the moment as I had lived no other to date.

CHAPTER 6

Pen Pals

During the mid to late eighties, I found myself consumed with collecting vintage drums, and more specifically vintage snare drums. I always believed that the older instruments were produced better than any of the modern-day instruments I was currently using. I found that the instruments of the 1920s and 1930s really lent themselves to the literature I was performing. Back in the day, most drums were constructed from a solid piece of wood to create the shell, or from one spun shell of nickel or brass, which was usually associated with a richer tone. The actual wires that ran along the bottom of the drum, known as snares, were made of gut in most cases, offering further darkness to the sound quality. These instruments were pretty easy to come by because there were very few collectors out there scooping them up. However, the vintage drum explosion was just around the corner.

I spent many hours (and many dollars) hunting for vintage drums. I scoured pawnshops, garage sales, and flea markets as part of my new passion. In addition, I had just been introduced to a very interesting trade paper called *Not so Modern Drummer*, a spinoff of the major publication *Modern Drummer*. Over the years, I had amassed a collection of more than sixty vintage snare drums. These drums were all unique, and some were more desirable than others, but all were wonderful in their own right. Some of the drums were made of metal shells, others from wood. They had that wonderful vintage dust and buildup packed nicely on their aged bodies and inner workings. With great enthusiasm I would clean each of these gems one at a time, bringing them back into playing condition. At times, getting the instruments back into playing condition took some real ingenuity and lots of detective work.

The process *after* acquiring the drum was usually even more difficult than finding the relic tucked in the corner of someone's junk pile at the local flea market. Once the transaction had been completed, I would need to take a full assessment of the drum and what parts may be missing after seventy-plus years. Using a drum key as well as a flat-tip screwdriver, I began my work.

Imagine you had just unearthed a 1920s snare drum, and now you see that the instrument needs a certain screw, washer, or some other moving part in order to attain two objectives: to complete the drum so it is in working and playable condition, and to bring the drum back to its original state at the time it was first assembled. This is no easy task because the local hardware store does not carry the type of hardware needed to recondition these babies. Many if not most of these drums have been reconditioned with parts that are readily available at Home Depot. I, on the other hand, am a purist and would only rebuild the newly purchased drum with authentic parts. That was part of the excitement in recreating history: looking for that special, one-of-a-kind thumb screw for some obscure drum made in some distant time.

It was in 1989 when I found myself in need of a tiny thumb screw for a 1920s Leedy drum. After exhausting all my normal sources, I learned that there was a man in Texas who was a sort of vintage drum guru. His name was Ray Benjamin. I learned that Ray was a resident of Kerrville and was indeed the man who could supply nearly any obscure piece for any drum. I dialed his number, introduced myself, and explained what it was I needed. He informed me that he had the missing screw. He assured me he would be sending it as soon as he could get to the post office. The total cost was $2.25—$2.00 for the screw, and $0.25 for shipping. Within a week, the screw arrived at my home in New Jersey. Along with the screw came a very nice letter of introduction, followed up by some questions concerning the particular drum I was working on. Ray's letter really moved me for some reason. I wrote a short letter of thanks and mailed it back to him at the address indicated on the envelope. Along with my thanks, I enclosed a photograph of the newly-restored drum, and thus our relationship was born. Shortly after my initial letter of thanks, I received a letter back from Ray with a word of thanks from him for *my* letter. This went on for a few months—mail exchanges from a man whom I had never met. I had the deep sensation of an unmistakable bond forming.

During our initial correspondence, we started adding sentences concerning our work, free time, and family. Before long, the letters turned from vintage drum talk to talk of family and life in a more serious vein. As our pen pal relationship grew, so did our concern for each other's welfare—not in the subtle sense, but in a truly heartfelt way that one may experience but once in a lifetime. All this with a perfect stranger! This stranger slowly but surely became part of my extended family. Together with his wife, Margie, they continued to share stories of tennis, God's work, recreational activities, drumming (for Ray, with the jazz combo), and of course his numerous trips cross-country in his beloved RV.

We began to write to each other on a regular basis, usually once a month. Our relationship survived decades of letters, most of which I have in my possession to this day. The only letters that I do not have copies of were hand-written letters I sent from overseas or some other remote location. During our years of writing, it was Ray who suggested strongly that I write down my stories of work, daily occurrences, and specific stories that I felt stood out from the norm. I took his advice and began keeping a detailed journal, of which now you are getting a glimpse.

Although many life changes have come to my dear friends Ray and Margie Benjamin, they are always with me, in my thoughts and in spirit. Excerpts from those letters that I collected over the years are still, to this day, thought-provoking and meaningful to me. I can see how, from letter to letter, our relationship grew and culminated in years of sharing family, life, death, work, drums, and lots of inner thoughts.

From the start, Ray wrote all his letters by hand—no computer, only pen and paper, the old-fashioned way. Each letter was on lined paper, like the kind we used while in grammar school back in the early seventies. So many memories would come flooding back with each letter I received from my pen pal. I do remember that in 1991, Ray purchased a personal word processor, but even after that he wrote most of the letters in his own hand. I still have all of them, and I love and cherish each meticulous ink stroke.

Here are some excerpts from our many letters.

> June 4, 1991, to Ray: "*When are you planning your trip to E. Canada? You know Eastern Canada is a mere 400 miles from New Jersey.*"

> October 23, 1994, to Ray: "*By the way, I do agree, one day we will meet face to face. I really look forward to it.… I am always in search of a better life and lifestyle—I am always pushing for new opportunities. I will always keep my eyes open for the unexpected. That is what truly helps keep me on my toes.*"

> December 11, 1994, from Ray: "*Success is measured by happiness, not by money or how many people you know, or anything of that nature.*"

Over time, I learned that Ray was significantly older than I. To this day I do not know his age, but I would place him about forty years my elder. This made the relationship all the more special on some level. He was the type of guy who would offer his advice to me, but in the most subtle way imaginable. His tactic was to compare his advice with a story of how the same circumstance surfaced during his life. He had a brilliant way of displaying reassurances to me, and by showing, leading, and teaching. He was able to do all this without making me feel he was jamming his convictions down my throat.

As 1995 approached, I began to see Ray and Margie's financial situation take a downward turn, for reasons unbeknownst to me. I was aware of this because the man who once supplied me with a simple two-dollar screw was selling off most of his collection. Let me tell you, he had one heck of a collection: over fifty instruments, all quality and all highly desirable. By now, vintage drum collecting was booming. There were shops springing up all over the map that dealt with this precise stock. Furthermore, the *Not so Modern Drummer* subscription went from two hundred subscribers worldwide to roughly two thousand members! People began to understand exactly what they had, and exactly how much someone else would be willing to pay for it. Snare drums made in the 1920s by William Ludwig would sell for two thousand dollars, when a few years earlier the same drum would fetch only two hundred. Buyers from all over the world were getting involved in the vintage drum craze, and many of our precious instruments would find themselves in China or somewhere in Europe. Many would find a new home with the top orchestras and recording studios throughout the world. I accepted the bittersweet feeling because I was happy to see the instruments were going to new homes with professional organizations. I was saddened because with each drum sold, my chances of finding another bargain were becoming more and more remote. As the desire grew worldwide to use vintage snare drums, demand rose and supply dwindled. With the ever-rising desire to acquire one of these instruments, the price tag soon followed suit.

Ray sold most of his drum collection to a prominent collector out west. I would imagine it was to help pay for life, because both Margie and Ray were getting on in years. I remember thinking, *Why didn't he offer to sell me any of his collection? Why would he leave me out of his massive collection?* Later I learned that the collector in Iowa offered him a considerable sum for the entire collection, and he would not make the offer a second time. Ray opted for the sure thing, and I couldn't blame him.

> July 7, 1995, to Ray: "*Ray, I take great solace in having such good friends like you and Margie. I would like to come and visit one day.*"

> December 7, 1995, to Ray: "*You are a true friend, Ray, and I do love you dearly for your friendship, understanding, and willingness to help.*"

> July 3, 1996, to Ray: "*The picture I chose to give you is me (of course) in Vienna at the Musicians cemetery. This cemetery is the final resting place for Brahms, Suppe, Wolf, Schubert, Strauss, and of course Beethoven. I was truly moved just to be there in their company. I found Budapest to be one of the most beautiful cities I have ever visited. Up north in Poland, Krakow knocked my socks off. I am really enjoying these traveling experiences.... I hope to make it to Kerrville one day soon. Stay well, my friend.*"

May 9, 1997, to Ray, referring to the Rudolfinum concert Hall in Prague: *"This is one of the most beautiful halls I have ever had the privilege to perform in. The stage itself is tiered so the percussion is above most of the orchestra, affording us to hear the slightest nuance… an incredibly sensitive venue housing centuries of history, you can feel it all around you. It feels as though the stage has a personality all its own."*

The following extract refers to my mother's passing on January 16, 1998.

January 24, 1998, to Ray: *"I wish I could write more, but am at a loss for words. I am glad to have you and Margie as friends, even long-distance friends. I need some time to pull myself together and deal with all that has happened over the past few weeks."*

The last time I had heard Ray's voice was when we first met so many years ago. After he received my very shaky letter of January 24 sharing with him the passing of my mother, he picked up the phone and dialed my number.

February 5, 1998, to Ray *"I was touched and moved to hear your voice on the other end of my phone receiver; it was just what the doctor ordered. You are a wise man, and I am still learning the ways of life from you."*

My and Ray's relationship had moved from drum talk with some small talk of life to letters of life and family with an occasional drum comment.

Letter to Ray on March 2, 2001: *As always I'm thrilled to hear from you, but am saddened by the news of Margie's illness. This must be a very difficult time for the two of you. I am sincerely at a loss for words.*

Ray, I am very concerned about you. Please tell me what is happening with your blood count, and how things have progressed since you last wrote. As you can see, "worry" gets us nowhere. Where did you get the reserve fuel (blood)? What type are you? In a heartbeat, I would offer you my friendship through any type of transfusion. I hope ours is a match.

March 2003: *"I have a story to share with you. Many years ago, you sent me a photo of all your famous "red" journals—volumes and volumes. The direct result of seeing that picture and reading your words to me, "Jim, you should keep a journal and write about all events and gigs," is that I have indeed kept a journal of sorts all these years. The publisher of the* Tower Revisited *(Seton Hall Prep's quarterly magazine) approached me and asked if I had any pictures of the countries I have visited, the gigs I have played, and so on. I told him not only do I have pictures, but I also have kept a half-assed account of the goings-on over the past decade or so. Since that day (about a year ago), he has been hounding me for some stories. I began to think that it might be a good idea to share with the alumni that the arts are still important, and one has to work very hard in this field. The days passed into months, and finally into a year. I began to sift through the endless pages I had written over the years. After coming up with a handful of stories, I printed them up and submitted them, along with a note explaining that I was not a writer! The stories are all in the first person; I wrote them as they unfolded and didn't pay too much attention to grammatical excellence.*

That is my story for the day, and I wanted to share it with the man who really helped foster the idea of keeping a journal: you, Ray Benjamin. I hope you enjoy the stories the editor printed and the spirit of music that lives in my soul.

Ray, I am dedicating this (my first) article to you, for your love and support through the years.

May 2003: *Perhaps one of your greatest assets has been overlooked? Did you ever consider your willingness to share in our friendship? I tell you, Ray, as sure as I am writing this letter, you have made a profound difference in my life. I relish the thought of years writing to each other and our commitment to the bonds of friendship itself. I have never met anyone before in my life who has taken such an interest in me, my work, and my life. I have been blessed many times over just knowing that Ray and Margie Benjamin exist, never mind being a part of their lives, no matter how small or large. I am grateful that we have had the time and desire to continue our long-distance relationship.*

I know I have been threatening you for many years about a visit to Kerrville, but I actually have the time to come down and really feel the need to do so. Please let me know if you have a few hours of time for me to make a short visit sometime this summer. I would like to come down in June if at all possible."

Letter to myself: *Get on a plane now ... Margie is sick.*

CHAPTER 7

Cluck-Cluck

It was in October of 1989 when I received a call to fill out the percussion section of a regional orchestra. The series of concerts were scheduled to highlight the great American composer, George Gershwin. I accepted the work. Once the roster was distributed, one of the members of the percussion section forewarned me that the conductor had the habit of laying into the new guy on the block, that he took great delight in testing the person's skills while attempting to unravel him or her. Over the years, the newcomer of this orchestra, no matter what section, was labeled the Chosen One. In this particular case, I was the new face in the orchestra—I was the Chosen One.

The piece in which I was called upon to perform was comprised of a large orchestra in which the percussion section utilized six players. I was hired to play the woodblock; nothing more. This particular orchestra was based out of state, a nearly three hours' drive south from my home in north New Jersey. I was employed for three rehearsals and four performances, and I wanted to make a good impression on my first day so many miles from home.

I arrived about an hour early to my first rehearsal, which is my customary practice. I began to unpack my duffel bag. It was filled with a half-dozen woodblocks of various sizes and pitches. In my mallet case there were two dozen mallets, comprised of the hardest of hard to the softest of soft. I brought with me what I thought to be a very thorough selection of woodblocks and mallets. This was my first appearance with this orchestra, and I wanted to have all my bases covered. There were a total of nineteen notes to play in this piece, and I wanted all nineteen notes to sound great.

I was set. All the woodblocks were sitting on a thick piece of black felt, ready to be struck. The felt I was using allowed the blocks to ring out as long as possible after being struck by any given mallet. Once set, I approached the principal percussionist and asked him his opinion on the woodblock of choice. We agreed on the block and mallet I would use. He was impressed with my overall concern for the music, and with the number of blocks I had brought for the rehearsal.

The personnel manager completed his routine announcements, and the rehearsal began promptly at 7:30 p.m. The conductor barely greeted the orchestra before he dropped his baton for the opening measure. I began counting the empty measures that preceded my part in anticipation of a good, clean entrance.

Four, three, two, one … and I was on. *Cluck, cluck, cluck,* I played. After the passage was over, the conductor dropped his hands to his side, signaling the orchestra to cease playing. He never said why he stopped, but he exhaled heartily and rolled his eyes. Once again, he lifted his baton, shouted a beginning point, dropped his baton, and we were once again off. Four, three, two one, here we go. *Cluck.* I never made it past the first note this time, when his arms fell lifelessly to his side. He folded his arms is disgust and began to shout at me. "Please, woodblock, please, warmer!" That was his entire statement: warmer. At least I received a "please." Without hesitation I switched mallets to a rubber-headed mallet, which was somewhat softer than my initial mallet of choice. This time when we began to play again, we started just a few seconds before my entrance. *Cluck!* The conductor stopped again. This time his eyes met mine when he shouted in a forceful tone, *"Warmer!"* This process happened four times; each time the vehemence in his eyes and voice grew stronger and louder, and each time I changed mallets and blocks randomly.

I recall looking at the principal percussionist as I shrugged my shoulders in disbelief. It was customary for the principal percussionist to answer for his section players, yet I received no help from the principal. I began to feel like crap. No support and no willingness to help out a colleague, a first timer, the newcomer, the Chosen One in the orchestra. I could feel the unrest within the orchestra personnel. Faces were all turned in my direction, waiting to see my next move. I remembered that this conductor was notorious for busting the balls of the new guy. I tried to keep these variables in perspective, but then I think I simply broke.

I began to sense that I might not get out of this one without doing something really radical and unorthodox. I took every wood block I had with me out of my bag and placed them on the table in front of me. I showed the conductor that I was a good boy and did indeed give a lot of thought to the passage I was to perform. After I lined up all the blocks, I emptied all the mallets out beside the well-placed woodblocks, further illustrating my willingness to offer him the best sound I could.

Now it was *my* turn to stare down the conductor and ask him what *he* liked. I changed blocks and mallets until I had no other possible combinations to use. I even tried a temple block with a timpani mallet, producing a sound like mush. That wasn't warm enough for this power-hungry master. This process carried on for at least five minutes. The conductor was so angry with me for not playing a warm enough woodblock that I could feel it well across the stage. I felt my blood pressure was reaching its boiling point. Soon thereafter, I came to the realization that I simply didn't care any longer about the outcome, and he knew it. I asked him, in front of my section and the entire orchestra, "Sing to me the sound you are looking for, Maestro."

That was the ultimate in disrespect, and he was speechless. I managed to put him on the defensive by not backing down. I put him in a place where he was uncomfortable, and with nothing more to say to me, he started to fidget at the podium. I grinned from ear to ear. With this smile, his eyes turned into little black beads of poison, looking right through me. His only comment was, "I still want it warmer. Can't you at least do that?"

I knew that I would never be permitted to play with this orchestra again anyway, and I figured I had nothing to lose. I shouted back a statement that was the final nail in my makeshift coffin. "Maestro, if you have a match, I can place it under the block. Perhaps that will be warm enough for you?"

At the intermission of that, my first rehearsal, I was dismissed for the remainder of the week. However, after he fired me, the personnel manager said, "On a personal note, no one has ever stood up to the maestro before. Bravo." With that, I packed up my woodblocks and mallets, and began the long journey home.

In all my years of schooling and professional experience, I never expected the events of that torturous October evening. It was something out of a movie. In case you are wondering, I was paid for all seven services for which I was originally hired.

CHAPTER 8

New Orleans

November 1992. November had been designated as "International Drum Month," which meant it is time for the annual Percussive Arts Society International Convention. The PASIC is the largest percussion event in the world, offering over 120 concerts, clinics, master classes, labs, workshops, panels, and presentations. It was also where colleagues and friends gathered and caught up on life, careers, and above all percussion talk. The three-day festival had been incredibly inspirational, and generally I would clear my schedule in order to attend.

In 1989, when PASIC took place in Anaheim, I met Fred Stafford from Atlantic Sticks. Fred and I were bidding on the same items during a silent auction, and during one particular auction we found that we shared the same likes, dislikes, and warped sense of humor. For the next several years we stayed in touch, and we have shared expenses by splitting our hotel room at future PASIC events. In 1992, Fred and I spoke sometime in September to solidify our November plans. As easy as can be, we reserved our room and once again agreed to split the cost. *New Orleans, here we come!*

The convention generally ran from Wednesday to Saturday, starting with an afternoon of contemporary music. The convention concluded on Saturday night with some spectacular musical event. We were booked for our four-night stay, Wednesday through Sunday. With our plans in place, I went about my normal business of practicing and preparing for the weeks to come.

A few days before boarding the airplane for Louisiana, I received a call from a local New Jersey contractor. I could hear in his voice that he was about to make me an offer for work, but I also detected some urgency in his voice. He began by saying that he had just received notice from the John Harms Theater in Englewood: a small ensemble was needed to back up comedian Joan Rivers. One rehearsal and two performances, all taking place on Saturday night—*this* Saturday. I told the contractor I had a conflict which I believed could be resolved. I asked him for a few hours to work it out, and he rejected me. He told me the fee for the three services and followed it with, "If you would like the gig, I need to know this moment." Of course I accepted and wrote the date, times, and the rest of the particulars in my trusty calendar.

I needed to call the airline and arrange an earlier flight home. This should be a snap: move the flight home from Sunday morning to Friday night. I dialed the airline and explained my situation. The representative was sympathetic and told me she would be happy to change my flight to Thursday morning. I persisted that I needed a Friday late afternoon or evening flight. I explained to them that I was arriving on Wednesday, and to come home on Thursday was not acceptable. While on the phone, it dawned on me I would need to pay for the hotel no matter what, because I had made arrangements with Fred a few months earlier. By moving to the Friday night flight, the cost of changing the ticket increased, due to the shortness of the stay. I was no longer including a Saturday night stay-over, which was how I had originally booked the ticket. It seemed like the agent wanted to help but had run out of options. The cost to change the flight was rising so much that between that and the cost of the hotel room, I would have spent more than half the fee I was offered to work the gig! Needless to say, I did not change my flight arrangements, but I did make a mental note that there was a direct flight from New Orleans to Newark at 9:45 p.m. Friday evening. I had a scenario building in my head, one that I wasn't sure was going to work.

On Wednesday morning, when I arrived in New Orleans, I made note of where the gate was in relationship to the ticket counter and exits. After recording the area with a snapshot in my mind, I jumped in a cab and headed to the Hyatt Hotel, home of the percussion convention.

While enjoying the events of the day, I ran into many friends from New

Jersey, as well as my once-a-year friends from all over the map. Among my Jersey friends was Patty. Patty was a fine percussionist, and over the years we had become good friends. We kept bumping into each other during the first hours of the convention, and finally we started to hang out together. By Wednesday evening, after all the exhibits had closed and long after the last notes of every master class had ended, we found ourselves in the bar, having a bite to eat and enjoying a beer. During this time, I explained to her how I needed to get home Friday night; I filled her in on the Joan Rivers gig as well. She listened in amazement that I had actually come to New Orleans without making the proper arrangements prior to my departure. I told her, "I have it all worked out; I have a plan."

We had a few more beers, after which we decided to play a quick game of pool. After all, we *were* in a sports bar, which was littered with competitive games. She beat mean the first game, and then the second and third. I said, "Let's shoot some hoops." She agreed and proceeded to beat me, three in a row. "How about shuffleboard?" Beaten three to nothing. I was getting discouraged, and we played a series of video games, all of which I lost. It was becoming an epidemic. No matter what we played, she beat me, and I don't mean by a little—she flat out kicked my butt. At that point, I ordered another beer, sat down, and said, "I bet I can drink this beer faster than you can drink yours." She beat me again. Patty was one tough cookie.

On Friday night, at around 8:00 p.m., I packed my bag, hailed a cab, and headed to Louis Armstrong International Airport. On the way, the cabbie regaled me with stories of Mardi Gras, and how many people generally die each year during the festival. It was an interesting topic. I listened with half an ear, because I was already beginning to plan my unconfirmed departure home. The show was about to begin.

Just after paying the fare and grabbing my bag, I began to huff and puff. I pulled my right shirt tail out from my pants, ruffled my shoulder-length hair and untied one shoe. Knowing exactly where the airline counter was, I headed over that way, but never actually made it. I began to wander around about twenty feet away, appearing to be disoriented. Because I had waited until thirty minutes before the last scheduled flight back to New Jersey, I stuck out like a sore thumb. Within a minute, a guard came to me, put his right hand on my left shoulder, steadied my wobbly body, and asked, "What is wrong, are you okay?" I told him I needed to get home immediately and couldn't find my airline. I was clutching the wrinkled ticket in my left hand, waving it to and fro. The kind guard steadied my hand to take a look at what airline I was using. "It is here, right in front of you."

By this time, the folks at the ticket booth were aware of the entire event. The guard led me to the ticket counter and explained how I was desperate to get home. At that moment, I yelled, "Her water broke—she is two weeks early!"

As the agent took the crumpled ticket from my hand, I was about to go into rich detail on how we had no family around us and she was all alone, but before doing so, the ticket agent said, "Okay, Mr. Neglia, we are all set. Now hurry to the gate because we are close to our departure time." I couldn't believe my ears. MGM—watch out, I was Oscar material!

In one breath I thanked her for all she had done and whisked myself away before they could change their mind, or wanted to charge me for the ticket change. I walked rather briskly away from the ticket counter and darted toward the departure gate, which I had memorized a few days earlier. As I reached the final check point I handed over my ticket. The agent looked at me and said, "Mr. Neglia?"

"Yes?" I replied.

"We have a problem."

My heart sank. I was a few feet from boarding the aircraft that would take me home. I lifted my chin from my chest and asked, slowly, methodically, "What is the nature of the problem?"

She said, "It's your ticket, your seat. We would like to offer you a first-class seat. We hope this will make your travel home more pleasant, and we wish you all the best with the birth of the baby."

"Why thank you," I said. "That is very thoughtful of you." With a nod of my head and a smile from ear to ear, I boarded the airplane. When I arrived through the door of the plane, the stewardess took me by the hand and settled me into my seat, tucking me in and offering me a blanket, slippers, and hot towel to cleanse my face from the city grime. A parade of stewards and stewardesses came to offer their congratulations, asking if this was our first birth, and if we had a name picked out. My head was about to explode when I graciously thanked them for their concern, but I needed to get some rest. Whew! I buckled my seatbelt, and a few minutes later we were cruising at thirty thousand feet.

Once home, life picked up where it had left off, with work and more performances. The Rivers gig was great, and everyone was happy. Over the weeks, during one of my various gigs, I ran into Patty and recounted the entire story to her, start to finish. Her jaw hit the floor, and although she was laughing at the situation and outcome, she told me, "One day this might come back and haunt you."

Jokingly I said to her, "It is over. I got away with one, and I will never, *ever* do that again."

Months passed, and the whole affair had long been forgotten when out of nowhere, my phone rang. It was the airline asking for Jim Neglia. "Um, that is me. How can I help you?"

"Well, Mr. Neglia, we were calling to see how the birth of your child went."

" Um," I said again, after gulping hard. "We are all fine, thank you for checking in."

"Yes, Mr. Neglia, you're welcome, but there is more—another reason for our call."

My God, my heart was now pounding harder. "What is the other reason for your call?" I fully expected them to say they needed a credit card number to pay for the fraud I presented back in November.

On the contrary, they were interested in hiring me and the baby to make a new commercial for the airline. They offered a considerable sum of money. It was an extremely tempting offer, but there was one problem—I didn't have a baby. After a ten-minute conversation where I declined their generous offer multiple times, the agent finally took no for an answer. He was really persistent and unrelenting, but in the final moments, I explained that it was against my beliefs to involve myself in a commercial. As I hung up the phone, I breathed a sigh of relief; exasperated, I poured a snifter of bourbon.

More than a year passed when I found myself on another gig with my friend Patty. We were performing a three-day series with three rehearsals and two performances. Having lots of down time during the program, we began to chat about our other work, and life in general. It wasn't until the second day we were together that she asked me about the commercial. She asked why I turned it down. I began to explain to her when it dawned on me: I had never shared that story with anyone. No one knew that the airline had called and made such an offer. It was at that moment that I knew that my friend Patty had played the ultimate prank on me.

To this day, I have been unable to get even with her, and I have resigned myself to the fact that she had beaten me again.

CHAPTER 9

The Tower

During the late eighties and most of the nineties, I spent a good deal of time traveling and performing in Europe. I wanted to document the day's events, and as a source of company, I would always travel with my reliable Palm Pilot. I took it with me everywhere, never knowing when I would sit down at a café to jot down my thoughts.

I never considered sharing my stories with anyone until I was approached by the alumni office at Seton Hall Preparatory. I had graduated from the Prep in 1981 and loved the school and all it represented. I thought long and hard about the desire to have my stories go public. In the final analysis, I thought it would be good to have the focus turn to the arts. I was hopeful that the article would serve as a reminder of how important music is in our lives. I felt it was not only my privilege but my duty to share these stories of a working musician—a sort of public service announcement for all to read. I agreed to send a chunk of journal in for review and consideration. As fate would have it, the editor of the *Tower* decided to include some of the stories in the spring 2003 edition.

When the publication arrived at my house, there I was on the front cover for all to see. This is when it hit me: this is for real, and the story has begun! It was both exhilarating and frightening. But what was even scarier was that my stories lay somewhere between the front and back cover. The interviewer compiled his notes from a series of documents I offered him, as well as one face-to-face interview in my home. Here is his article.

As regular viewers of PBS's Great Performances or Live from Lincoln Center, surely you've watched in awe, and perhaps a little envy, as the camera pans across the tuxedoed performers, so completely immersed in the music, their bodies swaying so totally in tune with the conductor, their faces so often aglow with feeling for the sounds they so elegantly produce.

Jim Neglia, SHP Class of 1981, gets to be one of those guys—a musician performing not only the work of the classical masters, but must know about every other kind of music possible. The refinement, manners and savoir-faire inherent to the career he has shaped over the last twenty years does, however, have a flip side. You've just as certainly watched in slack-jawed amazement at one of those hair-raising juggling routines, where the juggler keeps about seven objects in the air, including a bowling ball, a flaming baton and a chainsaw. Jim gets to be one of those guys, too.

As the founder and the prime mover behind his own music production company, and also a freelance percussionist, Jim leads an often-times frenzied life in the world he has pursued since his days at Seton Hall Prep in the late '70s and early '80s. His idea, formed in the early '90s: to provide "one-stop shopping" for anyone interested in presenting a musical experience to an audience. This "soup-to-nuts" company would take care of arrangements for the musicians, the contracts, the instruments, union relations, insurance, benefits, budgets, rehearsal arrangements, travel arrangements, payroll. Then, as a performer himself, he would also get to be on stage to do what he loves the most—play the drums, and any of about 50 other percussion instruments.

He must wear many hats, stroke dozens of egos and watch out for hundreds of details each week, all the while keeping sight of the beauty and art of the music he makes.

Like any of the hundreds of "freelancers" among the Prep community working hard to put food on the table, Jim stays ready, stays tuned in and stays networked. Luckily for him, actually through hard work and hustle, he also stays incredibly busy, with a schedule of work and travel that would make many a head spin.

Jim is president of Arts Alive! International Inc., a music performance and production company that contracts and provides musicians for the complete spectrum of musical and entertainment experiences. He has crafted a career that allows him to be a performer, contractor and manager of those musical events. He has gotten to rub shoulders with performers from every level of musical experience—from local performers at community theaters in New Jersey suburban towns, to the industry's superstars, like Placido Domingo, Jerome Hines, The Moody Blues and Andrea Bocelli. Quite a gig.

Jim's journals allow us to take a ride along with him on some amusing adventures.

This story takes place just six months before I began my current job, orchestra personnel manager of the New Jersey Symphony Orchestra. Here is more from the *Tower* interview.

The choices and challenges of a lifestyle and career like Jim's, like those of any freelancer, are counted by the score. In the world of music, balancing stability with the ability to work often is, as Stanley Tucci said, "a hard task." Jim has placed his work with the New Jersey Symphony Orchestra at the top of his "to-do" list. Few organizations offer freelancers retirement plans, health or instrument insurance benefits. These items become major expenses (no news bulletin to any reader), but especially for an independent contractor. Not so with the NJSO. So Jim is quick to accept their invitation to play. The downside is that other groups pigeon-hole him with the NJSO and sometimes skip over his name on the call list, figuring he's already busy.

So, networking is key. "To help combat the 'freelance dilemma,' I make certain to hire other freelancers who are high-profile players," Jim noted. "We eat, relax and perform well together, the perfect trifecta! I hire them and they recommend me for various gigs in and out of town."

His schedule boggles the mind; contracts and performances with ten to fifteen organizations, orchestra concerts, children's performances, chamber music and travel—sometimes two or three performances with different groups in the same day. "It can get confusing sometimes," he admitted. "Where am I going, what am I playing? Did I bring the right instruments? I hope the van doesn't break down."

For someone who learned the business-end of the game by jumping in with both feet, Jim manages to keep hold of the loose ends pretty handily. He described the non-performance side of a typical job:

"The steps I need to follow for each concert can be time-consuming, and always a bit frustrating. After speaking with the performing organization (administrators, conductor and managing directors), I learn what music is being performed. I then look up in my most trusted aid ("Orchestral Music" by Daniels) the actual instrumentation connected with the music being performed. Once I know the proper number of players needed, I work on the budget. The budget is presented back to the organization and either 'approved' or 'not approved.' If it is not approved, I've got to figure out ways to cut back the costs. (I do not like this part of my job.) Once all parties have agreed on the final number, contracts need to be sent, signed and returned to my office. The day the contract arrives in my hands, I begin to contact each musician. (E-mail has changed my life!)

"A normal-size orchestra consists of 70 to 80 players. Once all the musicians have been secured, I must send a list of player names and addresses to the 'librarian', whose job it is to send music to each player. With each rehearsal/concert, I must prepare a detailed letter to each musician. This information includes where the rehearsals/concerts are, what we are performing, dress code, contact numbers, drivers coming in (or out) of New York and, of course, the pay scale. Each local union carries their own criteria for payment. In New Jersey, I have three unions I work under, and I must know each and every rule/regulation imaginable connected with each local. In New York there is just one local for me to abide by.

"Health benefits, pension, and actual wages must be taken into consideration, as well as principal fees (leader of each section, violin, viola, cello, bass, flute, etc.). If a musician is called on to play more than one instrument, such as flute and piccolo, they receive another premium. As the rehearsal dates draw nearer, I am always sure to receive a few 'last minute' cancellations. More phone calls.

"Once the concert has been completed, I finalize the payroll, sending one copy to the local union, along with a contract showing dates, times and number of players. Another copy goes to the AFM-HB (American Federation of Musicians Health Benefit), another to the AFM-EPF (American Federation of Musicians Pension Fund); a third copy to the local union, showing the deduction of work dues along with checks for the amount indicated. I print up checks for each of the union requirements, and the musicians as well. I mail them out within 10 business days, and close the books on the event. What, I have to perform too?

"It is also my duty at each rehearsal to play 'time keeper.' It is on my clock that rehearsals begin and end, and on which all breaks are called. I synchronize my watch with the conductor prior to the start of all rehearsals."

CHAPTER 10

Passages

*"If you really want to hurt your parents, and you don't have
the nerve to be gay, the least you can do is go into the arts. I'm
not kidding. The arts are not a way to make a living. They
are a very human way to make life more bearable."*

—*Kurt Vonnegut*

I went through a great deal of hell while on the road to my chosen
profession. How much of it was absolutely necessary? How much of
the anxiety, fear, and uncertainty was brought on by others observing?
Most of the messages I received throughout my studies were about how
it would be impossible to make a living once I graduated from college.
Doctors and lawyers are also consumed with their studies, but somehow
they are in a real, viable, understandable field. Their chosen path has been
accepted by their peers as well as by society. The acceptance of those who
choose a more prestigious field, one that has a promise to make money,
is something of which we artists are acutely aware. We have had that
attitude rammed down our throats, starting from our early studies, and
it never lets up.

Education is the greatest gift society and our family can give us. Yet an
education in the arts is looked upon by the majority of people as a "nice
thing to do," as opposed to those of us who have a deeper understanding
of our particular need to express ourselves in our field. The message is
clear: studying music sounds like fun, but what are you going to do for
a living?

I hate to compare my path with others, but especially in the early days,

I found myself doing so. It was unavoidable and caused me a great deal of introspection. Only those in search of the truth can acquire true happiness. The search for some, including me, was very short-lived. My happiness came when playing or working toward performing; nothing more was required. I knew this from a very early age and never let go of the idea.

Many feel that musicians live an erratic lifestyle, one that doesn't conform to what society accepts or approves, which is a nine-to-five job, steady income, health insurance, pension plan, a 3-Series in the driveway, a wife, and two and a half children, not to mention the white picket fence. The perception is that musicians keep different (odd) hours than *normal* people, and therefore how can they live normal lives? We stay up late and sleep in. We work during the evening hours and on weekends, and we eat less-balanced meals than the average person. In reality, if you are one of the fortunate musicians who *is* able to land a job with a symphony orchestra, you will receive a salary larger than most nine-to-fivers, while working less than their forty-hour week. You will be offered a healthcare program, pension, and a 5-Series or better to take you to and from Symphony Hall. No picket fence required.

Student loans are a way of life for most, and I for one was always aware that one day I would need to pay this borrowed money back. Although I was one of the fortunate ones to receive a partial scholarship and was offered work studies while in school, I still managed to rack up a sizable student loan. A commitment of so many dollars per month for ten years was all it took to continue with my education; naturally, I signed the papers. I was reminded by those who were quick to point out that I should consider a second major, "Just in case your first one doesn't work out." They also felt the need to drive home what they thought were the facts, such as when a business major completes schooling and enters the work force, he will most likely get a job that offers him a good living and affords him enough money to pay back student loans to boot. However, when an *artist* graduates from school, his chances of finding a job are most precarious; will it even happen? Artists are looked upon as a risk, and even if they do find a job, they probably will not make enough to pay off their loans and live a life free of struggle.

In October 1990, while at my grandmother's wake, I sat in a chair close to the first row and stared at her. While deep in thought, I heard myself speaking; I was reliving memories, thoughts, and her words to me on so many occasions: "How is work?" "Where are you traveling to this week?" "Who are you performing with this season?" and so many other comforting questions. Rose was born in 1902 and raised two children; my mother and my uncle. She took extremely good care of them and played a large part in raising her grandchildren. She always seemed to have a handle on the latest events and what was happening with each of us, as well as the needs of our entire family. I have never known a more beautiful woman. She was lying there so peacefully, an empty shell of a woman who once gave us so much, never said no, and could make one heck of a tomato sauce.

While I was reminiscing, my cousin approached me. We exchanged mutual greetings, and soon the conversation steered toward work—my work. It wasn't long before he asked, "How are things?"

"Things are fine," I replied.

Somehow that was not the answer he was looking for. His real question should have been, "What are you doing these days to make money? How much do you make?"

We continued our charade of talking in circles until he finally asked the magic question. "What are you doing these days?" I began to explain about the various jobs I had successfully completed in the past few weeks. He was half-listening to the conversation, and half-thinking about what he was going to eat for dinner later that day. Every now and then I would hear, "Great, sounds good, how nice." After I finished my narrative, he then asked me, "So, how is your wife?"

"She is fine," I replied.

"Is she working?"

"Yes, at the office." With that statement he all but wiped his brow in relief. "That's great, so she has a job."

"Of *course* she has a job!" I exclaimed. He was relieved to hear that my wife was "supporting" me. I was not such a male chauvinist that it bothered me if my wife was making more money than I was. But the fact of the matter is that by that time, I was the major breadwinner in our home. The serious misconception people have of those of us in the arts. Just because I do not have "a" job does not mean that I do not have many jobs that sustain our lifestyle.

The implications and impact of being an artist were felt far and wide; sometimes it felt quite uncomfortable, even emasculating. Signing for a car loan was always tricky, because I never knew if I would need a co-signer. I recall purchasing both my primary home, as well as the beach house. The mortgage company demanded nothing short of blood tests to ensure that the monthly note would be met. Any loan I contemplated carried the burden of a million questions. Paperwork was provided showing income, taxes paid, a swollen bank account, investments, and a zero balance on all credit cards. Although armed with these supporting documents, the questions still persisted. The life I chose placed me in the vicious trap of financial uncertainty among the working class. This was an unfortunate aspect of life, one that took years to understand and ultimately conquer.

I wrote many times in my journal, "This is no walk in the park but a desperate, restless life which carries an enormous burden."

Journal Entry: June 21, 2003

It is our desire, energy, ambition, and absolute need for music in our lives that makes up our potential. One of the lucky ones, I never gave much thought to failure. Fear, yes; failure, no.

When our potential is nurtured by our elders, all becomes possible. Fortunate children have enthusiastic parents or guardians point this out to them at a young age. It is those who go before us who guide us upstream to our connected path.

Is it possible to confuse potential with raw talent? Raw talent being our God-given gifts. These gifts are what our parents may see as our potential. Once our gifts are recognized, then they may be transformed into what others see as our potential, and it is our parents who must recognize this quality in us and foster it.

Unnoticed gifts go … unnoticed, and therefore unexplored. It is possible that our gifts are seen, but those around us don't know how to act on or react to them, or even quite possibly even know they are supposed to act on them at all. If it weren't for our eager parents, aunts, uncles, and friends, some of our real potential would surely go unseen. For these reasons, I should be thankful to those who recognized my potential, my gifts, and helped take care of me during the process of developing to my fullest.

It was once said to me, "Change is always something you should fear." I responded with, "I think it is fear of not changing that we should be concerned with." Without change, how would we ever grow to our fullest?

I always felt like I was climbing a hill, having faced many challenges and hit some potholes, but always I got back up and continued on my course. Overcoming many adversities daily has helped me become a stronger, better person and musician.

I can see the beauty in the terrible and in the beautiful.

As a musician, we also bring beauty to the world. Through music I can help the audience around me transcend adversity, hardship, and grief. During a concert, for a few precious hours at least, we are able to help the listener be transported beyond their grief to a place of clarity and beauty. I thank God for all musicians and what they do for society; our music can help transport beyond the darkness of the most horrible days.

Self-Worth

"Being a musician is not a profession, it's not just a job, and it's not something occasional—it's the totality of your life and your devotion to something in which you believe profoundly."

—Isaac Stern

We musicians are not in the most lucrative field. Fortunately for most of us, money is not the most important item in our lives. Money to the average artist is needed merely for food, to pay the rent, and to maintain a particular lifestyle. I have noticed that non-musicians tend to live and work for money, just for money's sake. By living for and loving money, it causes them to be controlled by the almighty dollar itself. This is not how I wish to live my life; that is certain. I remember thinking about this in the mid '90s.

Journal Entry: February 2, 1996

People are motivated to make money to prove their own self-worth. As a musician, our self-worth is obtained while performing and expressing ourselves. Those who have never performed in an orchestra or danced on stage cannot fully understand the state of euphoria obtained when expressing our art form. It is the constant state of excitement we live in while performing that is at the root of our very existence. There is no dollar amount you can put on performing.

Thinking about our art form and how we express ourselves, I once compared performing music with that of painter's finished canvas. My thoughts gave me something to chew on for a while.

Journal Entry: February 4, 1996

Music, as we all know, is an "in the moment" event. As we perform, the events are unfolding. This is the true joy of live music and the art of performance. Once a concert is over, that's it; it's over. If you were not one of the lucky ones to have been part of the orchestra or audience on that particular day, you have missed it for good. Even recorded events lose the nuances of live music; the performance can never be recaptured, even if it was recorded using the best equipment available. The thought struck me: if a painter is unsure of their work, they have the option to shelve it or present it. It can remain on the shelf, along with other works never to be seen by the public. The painter can correct their creation without starting over. There is plenty of time to rework their image, fixing the fine strokes, adding shadings for more depth, removing a stroke that just did not appear where they wanted it. And if all else fails, at any given time the undesirable canvases can receive a fresh coat of white paint so a new image may emerge.

In music, we performers are out in the open, fully exposed. In some cases, we are performing works that have been performed for hundreds of years, works known by musician and audience alike. One misplaced note may resonate in a listener's ear indefinitely. We have no white paint to begin over. We are exposed in every sense of the word.

A painter has the luxury at all times to create and correct. If the image is not what they intended, they have the chance to fix it or simply start over. I find this option to be amazing. Can you imagine a musician telling the audience, "Let me try that again." Really, can you imagine that? This is why we spend endless hours in the practice room working on, among other things, muscle retention and consistency. At the end of a long day, I would fall asleep while I would hear the hypnotic click of the metronome in my head, long after the batteries have run out. This is the nearly insurmountable pressure we put on ourselves for doing what we like to do, or what we have been called to do.

> *"It is not impossible that out of a tremendous movement*
> *of amateur community music a peace movement could*
> *spread over the world ... People who make music together*
> *cannot be enemies, at least not while the music lasts."*

—Paul Hindemith

Journal Entry: July 7, 2003

Being an artist is a gift, but one that also carries a tremendous burden. It is not an easy life.

It is part of us; our music brings thoughts of climbing hills, compassion, love, grief, sadness, joy, and life. I think of my life as a gift, and as a burden as well. But now when I think about it, I have a deeper and better understanding of this burden. I believe the burden is our very own internal struggle with our gifts. Perhaps as a musician, we are more open to emotions, thus allowing our gifts to flow forth for all to see. There is nowhere to hide; all is in plain view. The fear that can sometimes accompany our performances due to exposure is part of our daily burden. Coupled with this concept, I feel it is necessary to carry these fears or anxieties into the performance world as long as it can be used to our advantage.

Remaining honest to oneself can sometimes come at a high price. In my case, honesty has taken the ultimate toll. Over the past several years, it became painfully obvious that my wife of nearly seventeen years and I had drifted apart—the end is at hand. Contributing factors to our demise were the daily hours I spent alone, dedicated to practicing, along with time abroad performing. In our case, absence did not make the heart grow fonder.

When I am performing, nothing else interferes with my role. While performing I remain focused, honest, and deliberate in my approach. The music before me, and blending with those around me, are the only thing on my mind. Nothing else can interfere. I am not performing a job or gig; I am not working—quite the contrary. I am immersed deeply; completely engaged and committed. This is when the music becomes flowing and effortless, part of my breath, part of my soul.

Concentration

Aristotle defined the purpose of art as catharsis, the vicarious trigger and release of emotion.

Journal Entry: July 9, 2003

When I am on, I mean really on, I have an infallible memory. I can recall where I was in my own thoughts during each work of a given performance for years to come. My memory will lock in on every stroke, nuance, passage, and performance offered. The upside of my memories is that I can use them as a growing tool for future performances, remembering (in fact knowing) what worked and what needs attention. The downside of my cursed memory is that I can torture myself for days, if not weeks, by pressing myself to overcome certain missed opportunities, phrasings, and offerings. After a gig, while on my way home or while lying in bed, the notes and passages are on constant replay in my mind. I could hear the volume of my playing in relationship to the ensemble, the performance level of the orchestra, the placement of each note, direction. Was I pushing, holding back, too much crescendo, too soon or too late? Like the curse of tinnitus, the passages never diminish from my mind.

Journal Entry: September 18, 2004 (after a performance of the Brahms Requiem while in the Slovak Republic)

The Requiem is musically strong, deep, thought provoking, and powerful in so many ways. It is as musically challenging as the text can be haunting. These thoughts caused me to spend this very lonely night in my bed, four thousand miles from home, shivering. During the performances I felt as isolated as one could imagine, and afraid of everything around me. As a result, my life, breath, heart, emotions, fears, pain, and anxiety were all rolled up in that single (recorded) performance. I expanded my musical and spiritual self into places I didn't know were possible, even while living and performing through it. During the second movement, "Die mit Tränen säen," I moved the low F triplet forward each time, propelling the orchestra as well as the text to a more exaggerated level. During the timpani baritone duet, "Denn alles Fleisch, es ist wie Gras," I chose to lay back more than I did in the dress rehearsal, playing a more supportive part to the singer. Once the chorus entered, I turned it up slightly, offering support to the 120 voices. Just before the finale of "Ich will euch trösten," I took the crescendo to new heights. Soaring high above the orchestra in harmony with the contra bassoon and basses, together we settled firmly from the dominant to the tonic. Glorious! During the "Ewige Freude" (Eternal Joy), I forced myself to hold back tears, measures before the start of the fugue. The text and orchestration all came together in one overwhelming offering. I am hearing the voice of God as broadcast by Brahms.

CHAPTER 11

Too Much Travel

"Everything in moderation, with occasional excess."

—Peart

Is it all glamorous?

Journal Entry: December 8, 1998

Back to the Czech Republic, Hungary, and Bulgaria: I have accepted a short concert series run in Central Europe.

Journal Entry: December 30, 1998, Sofia, Bulgaria, 11:00 p.m.

What a way to finish this year! This will go down as the worst New Year's Eve in my life. I am sitting in my "deluxe" hotel room, in the heart of Bulgaria. The accommodations include a bed the size of an army cot, a two-drawer dresser, and a thirteen-inch, black-and-white television set with horrible reception. However, the cockroach sizes are deluxe. The new year is less than an hour away, and I will be happy to see 1998 pass into history without any more problems.

While in Hungary a few days ago, I overslept and missed my scheduled train back to Brno. No one in the orchestra had bothered to ask where I was, because it was common for people to make their own arrangements from city to city. I missed the train by two hours and could do nothing about it. I called the reception desk to inquire if they knew when the next train was leaving. I was informed that the next train to Brno was departing in just under an hour. This meant I had about forty minutes to get from my hotel on the outskirts of the city to Keleti Pályaudvar station in downtown Budapest. If I left immediately, I just might make it.

When it comes to traveling, I bring only the essentials: tuxedo, toiletries, mini alarm clock, timpani mallets, passport, and money. I use a carry-on garment bag for my clothing and a small knapsack for my personal items, and I never put the two bags together. In the unlikely event of being robbed, at least the thieves would only get my tux and other clothes. After oversleeping, I only had about ten minutes to pack my belongings, hail a cab, and make the 12:45 p.m. scheduled departure to Brno. The train station was a good distance from the small suburb of Budapest, closer to Szentendre. So what did I do? In my rush, I packed everything together. Mistake number one.

Mistake number two was worse than I could imagine.

I arrived at the station with about five minutes to spare. Rushing through the doors, I quickly scanned the departures and arrivals screen to see where I needed to go. Over the years, I had acquired some basic but essential knowledge of the Czech language, but Hungarian is another story. All I could do was look for a track sign that advertised "Brno/Prague." I found it: track six. As I moved closer to the train, the final whistle blew. I was barely able to jump on board without falling beneath the iron wheels.

I had no ticket, but I had learned a little trick from my European counterparts some years earlier. Get on the train (no matter where you are going), and when the ticket collector comes to you and asks for your ticket, tell him you don't have one. At first he will look surprised, but you continue with, "Can I offer you some money for the ticket?" Without fail, the money is accepted and put directly into the pocket of the ticket collector. A fifty-dollar ticket will come out to about ten dollars on a bad day. On a good day, you can travel for as little as five dollars between countries.

My trip started in Budapest and made its first scheduled stop in Esztergom, a city in northern Hungary about forty-five kilometers northwest of Budapest. While there, the ticket punchers changed, as did the name of the country: Hungary became Slovakia. I explained my ticket issue. Two thousand Slovak Koruns (SKK exchange of about six dollars) passed from my hands to his, and off we went. "Welcome to Slovakia."

Next stop: Břeclav, a small town on the border between Slovakia and the southern Moravian region of the Czech frontier, approximately fifty-five kilometers southeast of Brno, my final destination. As we pulled into the station and the train came to a stop, I was awakened from a deep sleep. Somewhat disoriented, I still had my wits about me to immediately grab for my bag. Whew, there it was, right beside me. Hearing the musical motif that sounds when the doors are about to open or close, I rubbed the last of the sleep from my eyes. Lowering my hands, I noticed a guy staring at me; our eyes were locked. *Why the heck is he staring at me so intently? What is he doing?* I braced for anything imaginable, or so I thought. The musical motif sang out its song for the second time, signaling the closing of the doors.

At the last conceivable second, just as the doors were nearly sealed, this staring gypsy bum snatched my bag directly from my hand and in the same motion slipped out onto the platform. I leapt up to try to stop him, but the doors were already closed for our departure. I looked out the window of the moving train, only to see him darting up the stairs. As we pulled away, to add insult to injury, he turned and waved good-bye to me, just like that guy in *The French Connection*. I had been robbed! Everything was gone—everything! My clothing, tuxedo, my favorite mallets. I sat and sank deep, then deeper, into the seat. I still had forty minutes of torture to endure before arriving in Brno. Plenty of time to think about the violation I had just experienced. Plenty of time to relive the entire episode dozens of times in my mind.

A colleague from the orchestra met me at the train station. As we walked from the platform, I launched into a pained, detailed explanation of all that had happened from the time I woke up to the time he met me at the station. The more I spoke, the further his shoulders sank. He was filled with compassion and empathy for my situation, but he had very little to offer as far as a remedy. With little more to discuss, he took me to a rental shop just outside of the city to pick up a tuxedo for the evening concert. Afterward, we went to a local music shop, where I was able to purchase some timpani mallets. While there, I reached into my inner coat pocket and, thankfully, found my money clip, credit card, and passport. The Slovak bum didn't get everything after all. It was also my standard practice to separate my Palm Pilot and its folding keyboard into a safe, accessible place, so thankfully I still had it with me. I thought of my Palm Pilot as a true companion, because it traveled with me everywhere, carefully taking notes on all I did.

That night while in Brno, I played the concert with tears in my eyes. I saw again and again the look on the face of the thief. I can still see him laughing at me. After the performance, when I arrived back at the hotel, I cursed out anyone and everyone I could for leaving me in Hungary. Down in the lobby, I purchased a toothbrush and some toothpaste and then stormed off to my room, mostly angry with myself.

The next day, we boarded the airplane and flew to Bulgaria for a New Year's Eve performance in the heart of Sofia. The performance took place at Zala Bulgaria, located on Shipchenski Prohod Boulevard.

Journal Entry: January 1, 4:00 a.m.

I am watching my TV, my little TV, tuned to CNN (one of six fuzzy channels). I watched the new year celebration in four time zones. At 7:00 a.m. local time, I will call home to send my love and good thoughts to my family.

Journal Entry: January 1, 7:45 a.m.

Modern technology has not yet crept into Bulgaria. The lobby phone is plagued with static and disconnects every thirty seconds. I've spent the past half hour trying to call the States. After a dozen attempts, I finally was able to say hello, and pretty much nothing else.

Journal Entry: January 2

There is absolutely no point in hanging around Europe another day. I want to go home. Last night I realized that my airline ticket from Prague to the United States had been among the items stolen. It can't get any more depressing than this.

Later that evening:

I am back in Prague after an uneventful flight. Called Czech Air to reschedule my flight home. I am out of here now! So much for staying in town to decompress. I am going back home to lick my wounds.

After calling CSA and informing them of the stolen ticket, they requested that I arrive at 7:00 a.m. to have them reissue it. I am to arrive at 7:00 a.m. for a 12:25 p.m. flight. I couldn't believe my ears and thought for sure that it was my lack of understanding the Czech language, but no, in Czech and English, it all translates the same: get your ass to the airport by seven to ensure that you will get a seat on the only direct flight home.

Shortly after receiving my 6:00 a.m. wakeup call from the front desk, I asked them to call a taxi for me, and off I went. When I arrived at Ruzyně Airport some twenty-five minutes later, I darted to the CSA airline counter. The woman at the ticket counter listened attentively to my part Czech, more than large part English, story of robbery, fear, and desperation, with what I must admit was the look of real understanding and compassion. Unfortunately, she also needed to inform me that my business-class ticket could not be reissued because there were no empty seats on today's flight. She went on to explain that if I wanted to get on the flight today, I would need to sit in coach and pay the twenty-five-dollar reissue fee.

Only one flight per day departs at 12:25 p.m. from Prague back to Newark, and that is Flight 052, which I nicknamed Old Faithful. With feelings of total desperation and dejection, I felt I had no choice but to get on that flight. I guess I could have waited another day and sat in my accustomed seat, but I really needed to get home; I needed to feel something other than desperation and misery. Furthermore, I needed a fresh set of clothes—I had been wearing the same set for the past four days. (I did purchase another pair of underwear, in case you were wondering.)

I had to kill four and a half hours before even thinking about boarding the plane. What was there to do? I had a small bite to eat, drank coffee, and looked at the newspaper, of which I could understand only about every seventh word—useless. I walked to the newsstand, looked for a book to read, and purchased some gum and hard candies for the flight. Only twenty minutes had passed. Christ, I would lose my *mind* if I couldn't find something to occupy my time.

While walking around the airport and staring at people, I played a game with myself. I tried to guess what the people in the airport were thinking and where they were heading. Was it for work or holidays, were they in business class or coach? This proved to be a complete waste of time, because the fate of everyone I guessed may or may not have been correct! And on top of that, none of them were robbed of their business-class ticket and dignity a few days earlier. Another twenty minutes passed.

During this period, gambling was permitted in most of Europe, and many mini casinos were available in the international airports. I passed by the entrance of the Ruzyně Casino and stopped for a moment to think about my next move. I still had hours to kill and convinced my mind to accept the fact that over the past few days, I had been mentally and emotionally beaten to a pulp. Therefore this *must* be my time to win, win, win! I entered the small, enclosed area and presented my passport for verification. I glanced to the left and right and found a table I thought would be fun, entertaining, and lucky. As I sat down, I could feel the downward spiral about to turn around. I reached into my pocket and pulled out a handful of Czech koruna. Slowly and in measured amounts, I began my play, strategically placing my well-calculated bets in the proper places. In a matter of minutes, I had no money remaining in my stack or in my pockets. Still more than two hours remained before boarding would be called. I decided to cash in some US dollars so I could lose—I mean, play—some more. The same sequence of events took place, and before I knew it, I was broke. I did not even have enough money to purchase a cup of coffee or a piece of toast.

I walked out of the casino in a greater state of depression than when I first walked in. Was this really happening to me? Was it possible that I had pissed off the gods of travel so much that they were taking their revenge out on my poor soul? Couldn't they just back off for a while and let me be?

I walked the airport for the next seventy-five minutes or so, making circle upon circle, so much so that I am sure some people were watching me thinking I was some crazed moron with nothing better to do. I remember walking in those crop-circle motions thinking, *I want to go home! Please let me go home.* Near tears, I finally heard the most beautiful announcement one could imagine: "Now boarding Flight 052 to Newark." Sweet success! I had made it back from hell and was now on the road to heaven.

I patiently waited for every passenger to board the airplane before I passed the ticket area. I was the final passenger to board Flight 052 back to Newark. As I passed my normal seat, 2A in business class, I began to scan the aircraft for the empty seat in coach. My eyes could not find a single seat anywhere on this jumbo airbus. Were there any at all? No, there it was, in the back row—actually, the last row where the seats don't recline at all. Moreover, I was in the middle of a three-passenger-wide section.

As I advanced to the last row, I noticed that my seat partners must have been brothers. They shared at least two common bonds: Neither one of them believed in bathing, and neither one of them believed in pushing himself away from the dinner table. These were two massive individuals. I inserted myself in between the two ponderous bodies that surrounded my seat. I had to turn my shoulders sideways to get beyond halfway down. Was this really happening? For the first time in days, a funny thought popped into my head. I should ask the stewardess for some butter to spread on myself, to help slip down between Tweedledee and Tweedledum.

The stewardess was yelling at me to buckle my seatbelt because we were ready to begin taxiing for takeoff, but I couldn't get near it. There were pounds of blubber all around me, and I was sure some of it was covering a portion of the seatbelt itself. What did it matter? If the plane went down, the massive forms surrounding me would certainly protect me from any harm. I called over the same stewardess who had just yelled at me, and I asked her if there were any other empty seats. She retorted sharply, "Only the one you are sitting in, and that will be vacated soon if you don't fasten your seatbelt!" Somehow I was able to pull my seatbelt out from down below and fasten it around my waist.

We sat at the gate for what seemed to be an interminably long period of time; I can't tell you exactly how long, because my damn travel clock had been stolen. I found out later that we were delayed because a light would not go off over the door. A light? Are you for real? Change the fuse, and I bet it will work. It took all of two hours for the masterminds to figure out how to make the light go off.

Once airborne, it would be another grueling ten hours before we were to arrive at Newark International Airport (now Liberty International). Every second seemed like a year, and I was beginning to unravel quickly. I began thinking of ways to occupy my time, but I could not move my body to even pick up a magazine to read, because the fat brothers had released their girth into my chair, placing undue pressure on my miserable existence.

In a moment of real weakness, I took a deep breath and began bargaining with God, begging my maker, *Please make the trip go quickly. I won't curse anymore, I will be good to my brothers and sisters. I'll try to go to church every week. I will stop thinking bad thoughts of these fat slobs who occupy my space.* God must have been asleep or on vacation, because as the trip progressed, the two brothers began to really stink up the entire back of the plane. I am not sure what or who they ate before boarding, but something had exploded in one or both of them. As they got more comfortable, their bodies oozed over into the middle seat—*my seat.* It was like they were melting onto me, and there was nothing I could do to save my life. Drowning in their blubber, again I began bargaining with God, pleading my case, asking for forgiveness. But again God must have been busier with those who really needed more attention.

I couldn't take it anymore. After pushing my way out from under the stench of lard and whatever those fatties had eaten hours before, I begged the stewardess to let me sit anywhere else, or let me just stand for a while. The cruel stewardess allowed me to stand in the aisle next to my seat. No problem, as I was in the last bloody row anyway. I was not in my comfortable business class seat, where I would have been at a forty-five-degree angle, wearing slippers, covered with a blanket with a pillow under my head, and a full stomach.

While standing there, looking out the window into the cloudless sky for eight and a half hours, I didn't eat. Who could, with the reek that surrounded the entire area? I didn't drink anything, either, and my feet were killing me. In less than twenty-four hours I had flown from Bulgaria to Prague and from Prague to the United States. I had slept a total of six hours in the past three days, and I was too stressed to even give a damn. In addition, I had been robbed and violated, although I was feeling like the *real* violation was in the loss of my comfort zone in seat 2A. I must have been one hell of a bad guy at some point in a past life, because this flight lasted what felt like twenty hours.

There is IKEA, so where is the airport? There it is. Thank you, God, thank you! You heard my promises never to curse again! Wait, what the heck is going on? After traveling as much as I did, I knew exactly what was happening: we were circling the airport. This could go on for a while, or the rest of my natural life. Hopefully my agony would soon come to an end.

The plane finally touched down, and we rolled in at a snail's pace toward the terminal. Within a microsecond of the seatbelt sign going off, I sprang up and started my dash for the door. I made it all of three feet before the couple of hundred people in front of me also jumped to their feet in unison. I had forgotten how people in coach react to a ten-hour flight. (Sorry, that sounds so snooty.) In business class, I would just now be taking off my CSA slippers and replacing them with my shoes that had sat to the left of my oft-used seat. I had been the last to get on the plane, and I was just about the last to get off. I swallowed and even accepted my fate, because at least I was now in Newark and just a short drive to my home in North Arlington.

The parade of slow-ass people taking their carry-on luggage from the overhead dominated the final minutes of my wretched existence. Once again I accepted it, because I could taste my home just nine and a half miles away. What felt like an extraordinary amount of time to get off the plane couldn't have been more than ten minutes total, but it felt like another hour.

Finally, I was in the terminal. Because I had nothing to claim, I realized that I didn't need to go to baggage claim. Ah, the silver lining of this infinitely black cloud. Instead, I ran to the customs line. *Nobody in front of me? Holy crow, is it possible?* I showed my passport, received a Newark stamp of acceptance, and headed to the declaration line. I could feel the water of the hot shower waiting to wash the day's grime from me. I could smell the sheets on my own bed!

I had no parcels to declare, so this should be a snap. The declaration official asked the normal questions (how long were you gone, where did you visit, etc.), and then he asked to examine my luggage. With only a fanny pack in my possession, I explained the story of my stolen case and situation. He said, "I understand, but let me see your luggage." With that, I once again told him of my situation; this time I also offered him the explanation of the stinky brothers whose blubber had surrounded me for the past dozen or so hours, and how if I didn't go home soon, I would indeed implode.

He still didn't believe that I had no luggage. Nothing I could say would make him believe me. With seemingly nothing to lose, I said, "If you want to detain me, you will need to arrest me. If not, get out of my way." Like in a scene out of the movies, the hero got away with that one. I was, after all, owed at least one.

CHAPTER 12

Opportunity Knocking

Journal Entry: July 18, 2001

There is an old saying: it is not what you know, but who you know. Over the past few years, some opportunities have come up simply because I was in the right place at the right time. Here are the details of one of those happy occasions, where everything seemed to fall into place without too much effort and worry.

While on break from a double rehearsal at Lincoln Center (Ludwig Minkus' *La Bayadère*), I was having lunch with a friend on the corner of Broadway and Sixty-fourth Street. It was then that his cell phone rang, and his phone call became *my* new best friend. As he began his conversation, I kept eating (what was I supposed to do?). About a minute passed without any verbal response from my friend, then a barrage of yes's followed. I put the fork down; he had my full attention. The call was from Mayor Giuliani's office; they sought help in putting together a concert in recognition of those who helped get the mayor reelected. Let the celebration begin!

Journal Entry: July 29, 2001, "The Mayor"

I performed a wonderful concert with Amor Artis Chorus (based in New York City) with guest conductor Rudolph Giuliani. I was asked to take over the responsibilities of this event due to a previous commitment by my friend and colleague. This was a special concert that was to feature the original version of Handel's *Royal Fireworks*, a work rarely performed in its original scoring. A normal orchestra calls for double woodwinds, meaning two flutes, two oboe, two clarinets, and two bassoons. However, this version of the *Royal Fireworks* music calls for twelve oboes, ten bassoons, two contra bassoons, six trumpets, six horns, two percussionists, and one timpanist. This was really quite amazing in scope alone, and I knew once musicians learned that I was booking this event with this work being performed, the appropriate people would come out of the woodwork to participate. Heck, they may even pay *me* to let them play!

The *Royal Fireworks* were being featured on the second half of the program. The first half of the program consisted of opera excerpts requiring a full, symphonic-size orchestra. The total number of musicians needed is sixty-two, including the harpist. Through my affiliation with Amor Artis (as their principal timpanist), and the conversation that took place on Sixty-fourth Street during lunch, all agreed I should be the point man of this event.

The first order of business was to call Mayor Giuliani's office and settle all the arrangements. First on my list: the money needed to pay the musicians about to be hired. Once I had secured the funds for the performances and received a signed contract, I needed to secure all the musicians as quickly as possible. It was the summer, and most of my first-call players were away performing at festivals all over the country and world. The mayor's office contacted me just a day and a half later, requesting all the names of the musicians for security purposes; they wanted the list as soon as possible.

Along with hiring all the musicians, I had a long checklist of other important items to attend to. I needed to secure a rehearsal location for the event and parking for guests, rent all the percussion instruments, prepare letters of information for each player, and file the paperwork with Local 802, the New York Musicians Union. The only part of the event that had been taken care of by the mayor's office was the concert venue itself: we were to perform at the Richmond County Bank Ballpark, in Staten Island.

There were to be two two and a half-hour rehearsals, a one-hour sound check at Richmond County Bank Ballpark, and the performance. We'd have our first rehearsal on July 23 from 3:30–6:00 p.m., just five days after receiving the initial phone call. I wanted everything to go well for the mayor, as well as the music director of Amor Artis, Johannes Somary. I was extremely fortunate in the hiring process, because this was a high-profile job, and nearly every musician I called accepted the opportunity on the spot.

The first rehearsal was set to take place at the Blessed Sacrament School on Seventieth and Broadway. The school donated their space for the event free of charge. I was able to procure a few dollars honorarium for them as political thank-you; everyone was happy. I arrived several hours before the beginning of rehearsal to check out the location and deal with any unforeseen problems. What became plainly obvious within the first five minutes of my arrival was that there was one major problem that I hadn't considered: there was no air conditioning in the rehearsal hall, or the entire building for that matter. This particular week in New York City, we were dealing with a blistering 94 degrees and 85 percent humidity.

In addition to all the details laid out thus far, I was responsible for supplying all of the percussion instruments, including three timpani, bass drum, and anvil, as well as other requirements for the event. As a percussionist and timpanist, I am always looking for the easiest, most convenient way to get in and out of any room, no matter where it is located or on what floor. Lady luck took a back seat today, as I soon learned that the rehearsal was set to take place on the second floor. This was a very old-style school with small elevators. The elevator was so tiny that it was not possible to fit even my smallest timpani. I had to take all three timpani up the fifteen steps to the rehearsal room, one at a time.

The other problem was that I was on my own, so how was I going to take these instruments up a full flight of steps alone? The answer: find someone on the street and offer them fifty dollars to help me out. That is precisely what I did. I approached the first young, energetic lad I spotted and literally placed a Ben Franklin in his hands, saying, "If you help me get this vanload of equipment up to the second floor, you can keep it." I went on to make the following offer. "If you return at 6:00 p.m., there is another fifty with your name on it." The young man accepted, and sure enough, he returned at 5:55 p.m. to collect on my promising offer.

At precisely 3:29 p.m., I stood up in front of the orchestra and asked the concertmaster to tune up. Before I was able to greet the group and tune, some of the musicians were complaining about the horribly hot conditions in which we had to work. I explained that I was working on it (which was a total lie), but then I gave it further thought and came up with a solution.

We tuned and began our rehearsal promptly at 3:30. As soon as the rehearsal began, I called for the custodian, gave him some money, and asked him to purchase three oscillating fans. Fifteen minutes and thirty dollars later, there was a damp breeze circulating through the room. The gesture was greatly appreciated by all.

This was the day that the mayor of New York City was to arrive and conduct the orchestra. The mayor was set to arrive at 5:00 and conduct the famous "Anvil Chorus" from Giuseppe Verdi's opera *Il Trovatore*. I had prepared the orchestra regarding the mayor's appearance, and they were all waiting with excitement as well as professional behavior. Even though the air was thick, moist, and at best uncomfortable, the atmosphere in the room was totally electric. We were all waiting with great anticipation for the mayor's arrival.

For each of the two and a half hours of designated rehearsal time, our musicians are required a twenty-minute rest break. I scheduled this specifically with Maestro Somary to happen at 4:35 until 4:55; it should work perfectly. At 4:55 p.m., while the concertmaster was tuning the orchestra, I heard a scuffle at the bottom of the steps. The mayor had arrived.

As the "A" died down, and just before the honorable mayor entered the room, there was an entourage of photographers, journalists, reporters, and of course a handful of Secret Servicemen filing in. Once these folks were assembled and had taken their appropriate places, the mayor made his grand entrance. He walked in with an air of authority and competence. Johannes greeted him with open arms. Giuliani was offered the baton immediately, but he declined and asked if the orchestra would first play a selection, so he could listen and enjoy the moment. Of course we accommodated him. Mayor Giuliani began to applaud loudly after our selection was over. He was extremely receptive to the orchestra, the conductor, and all involved in this production.

Johannes asked Mayor Giuliani if he was ready to conduct the "Anvil Chorus." Without pause, the mayor tilted his head in acknowledgement. The opening of the "Anvil Chorus" is not tricky for a veteran conductor, but for a novice it could present a problem. Without missing a beat, Johannes started the orchestra off, and seconds later, he passed the baton to Giuliani. He was having a blast! His face, demeanor, posture, and enormous smile told the complete story.

About thirty measures into the piece, I have to play a few triangle notes in rapid succession. As I began to perform these notes, the mayor looked at me with a smile from ear to ear. But the real fun was about to begin. Twenty or thirty short measures later, I came clanging in with the famous anvil part that gave this chorus its name. For this particular selection, I chose to use two brake drums from a 1984 Dodge Caravan. The mayor looked at me, astonished. As I began to hit my anvil, the media, photographers, and journalists gathered around. While I was performing, they were asking, "What is that?" While playing, I began to explain to them the significance my part had in this particular piece. They began jotting down notes in their small spiral notebooks to use later for *Today's News*.

After Mayor Giuliani was finished conducting the selection, and the orchestra shuffled their feet in appreciation, he came to me and asked me whether he could have a quick lesson on my anvils. Naturally I obliged him. The anvil is played with a regular ball-peen hammer, stroked with great force to produce the effect required. When I picked up the hammer to show the mayor, I began to raise the hammer over my head. With that, the Secret Service grabbed at my arm, apparently thinking I was going to bludgeon the mayor. They stopped me mid-stroke. My heart jumped into triple time. The mayor smiled and told his protectors all was fine, and that I wasn't going to hurt him.

Let the lesson begin! The camera bulbs began to flash, one after another. A ten-second lesson turned into ten minutes of conversation. Afterward, the mayor gave me a firm handshake and a fine sendoff to the day's events. I was so proud, excited, and somewhat overwhelmed. I wasn't amazed that he took a few moments out of his busy schedule to enjoy and conduct classical music—it was the mini-anvil lesson that blew me away.

I was sure to remember to pack my camera for this event, and I asked one of the photographers if they wouldn't mind taking a picture of Mayor Giuliani and me as a keepsake. I was so excited to have a photograph of the mayor for my private collection and website. I kept thinking to myself, *What great publicity! I must remember to bring my camera to the concert on Staten Island as well.*

It was my duty to make everybody feel at home, and that included the musicians as well as the mayor and his entourage. The reporters were asking me many questions, all of which I answered with direct and short "sound bite" answers. Many of my colleagues told me that I was in rare form and was really working the room. It was from this day on that my nickname among this crowd became The Mayor.

On July 24 we had our second rehearsal. This rehearsal went off without a hitch, and even the weather cooperated. On July 25 we had to travel out to Staten Island, to the home of the New York Yankees' minor league ball club. The stage was set up in the middle of the playing field, right over second base. There were huge pillars of lights shining on the orchestral stage, as well as one of the largest sound systems I had ever seen. In center field there was a large screen that carried the concert event. This was great for close–ups. On with the show!

We played many selections that evening, under the same conditions we had on July 23. The weather on this particular evening hit a record 96 degrees, with near 100 percent humidity. Why it wasn't raining was a mystery to me. We were waiting for the rain to come, and eventually it did. We performed for about an hour, and shortly before the scheduled intermission, the sky opened up. The orchestra was calm, but with great focus and speed, they exited the stage, hoofing it to the dugout to take shelter.

Once the rain passed, we took to the stage—or shall I say field—again. We played a few more selections before the man of the hour was announced. The mayor was to take up the baton for the next selection. "Ladies and Gentleman, the mayor of New York, Rudy Giuliani." Giuliani came running out from the dugout wearing his Yankee jacket and cap. As he reached the stage area, he quickly switched into his suit jacket to conduct the "Anvil Chorus." Before he began to conduct, he glanced over at me and looked for the now-famous hammer. With camera and hammer in hand, I began inconspicuously snapping pictures of the event. Great memories!

Before the last note of the music had a second to die in the damp air, the applause exploded over the stadium. The mayor was indeed a hit. From his podium, he motioned to the orchestra in acknowledgment; we all stood up to take a collective bow. With the orchestra on their feet, we gave him a round of applause back for having the chutzpah to get up there and actually conduct us. Before the mayor exited the stage, he ran over to the percussion section and asked me for another quick lesson on the anvils, this time in front of the entire audience. Once again the mayor and I had an exchange of musical thoughts. After this brief lesson, he shook my hand in gratitude, and I embraced him as a new friend and percussionist. I presented him with the hammer that I used for this concert, and he accepted it graciously.

The remainder of the concert went off without a hitch. We performed one or two more arias and moved into the *Royal Fireworks* music. During *Royal Fireworks*, actual fireworks lit up the sky behind the stage. Sight and sound—our senses were totally engaged. It was truly a magical evening, and I was thrilled to be a part of it. I have no memory of packing up my instruments and driving home after the concert.

The *Staten Island Advance* writes,

> It's a wrap! In honor of the residents of Staten Island, and their support for Mayor Giuliani, a concert was held at The Richmond Bank Ballpark on July 25, 2001. The Mayor had requested many of his favorite opera excerpts, which included Puccini's *Nessun Dorma*, Verdi's *Brindisi*, Bizet's *Carmen Suite* and the famous *Anvil Chorus* from *IL Travatore* by Giuseppe Verdi. With great appreciation and commitment to classical music, Mayor Giuliani took up the baton to conduct the *Anvil Chorus* himself. The Grand Finale of the evening featured a performance of the *Royal Fireworks* by G.F. Handel in its original instrumentation: 12

oboes, 10 bassoons, 2 contrabassoons, 6 horns, 6 trumpets, 2 percussionists and a timpanist. Arts Alive International, Inc. wishes to thank all who were involved in this festive event: Johannes Somary, conductor and music director of New York City's own "Amor Artis Chorus," the stage crew, grounds crew and management of The Richmond Bank Ballpark. Mayor Giuliani's staff, media, entire entourage and of course Mayor Giuliani himself, were most gracious. Very special thanks to New York's finest musicians, who performed at the highest level attainable."

CHAPTER 13

Comissiona

"In the practice of tolerance, one's enemy is the best teacher."

—Dalai Lama

In November 1999, the Romanian-born Sergiu Comissiona came to conduct the New Jersey Symphony Orchestra in four performances of Gustov Holst's *The Planets*. The orchestra was filled with anticipation and excitement. I wished I was able to share in their excitement, but I couldn't. My relationship with Comissiona had been tainted some years earlier.

In December of 1987, while finishing my master's degree, Comissiona came to guest-conduct our school orchestra. We were performing the great tone poem *Don Juan* by Richard Strauss. At the time, I was the timpanist with the orchestra. I was eager for the opportunity to perform under the baton of the great Comissiona, was extremely confident in my preparation, and knew what I wanted to do with the timpani part. I had just performed the work a few months earlier with a freelance orchestra, so I was very comfortable with the situation.

Unfortunately, the day the reading was to take place, I woke up with fever of 101 degrees. Not wanting to miss this incredible opportunity, I dragged my butt out of bed. I jumped in the shower, got dressed, and went to school as any other normal day. On the trip into the city, all I could think about was that for us timpanists, our ears are our lifeline to the rest of the orchestra; fine-tuning is essential. Blending with the rest of the orchestra is an absolute requirement. All the while, I was brainwashing myself to believe that I was fine, not giving way to my fever and obvious congestion. I was clogged, sniffling, sneezing, aching, and half-deaf from the combined symptoms. My hearing was a real mess. I knew it but pretended otherwise. It became apparent when I put the radio on 1010 WINS to hear the current traffic pattern. It sounded as if Judy DeAngelis was underwater, inaudible, and almost smothered in tone.

During the car ride, my thoughts shifted from the news to the Strauss. There were many pitch changes in the tone poem, all of which required spot-on tuning. The start of the work was filled with excitement, a dazzling display of sixteenth notes propelling us headfirst into Don's world—and, in my opinion, effectively conveying Lenau's poem. In the middle of the work, Strauss includes a very beautiful and passionate section of music that highlights the principal oboe; this is known by all who have performed the work as the wonderful love-making section. The act itself is depicted in the gorgeous melody performed by the oboe. The oboe's lyrical solo is supported on the bottom by the timpani. Here the timpani are not used to punctuate the music; rather they create a warm base of sound that needs to be placed and tuned precisely to perfect fifths (low G and D above) with the contrabasses.

Before rehearsal began, I was careful to warm up, mostly by tuning and retuning the timpani to all the required pitches in the work. I spent the better part of the hour tuning and retuning. While checking myself along the way, I felt confident my hearing would hold out for the hour and a half rehearsal. I felt prepared, ready, and excited to begin. At 1:00 p.m., the orchestra assembled, we tuned, and off we went. Comissiona said nothing as he jumped onto the podium. He picked up his baton and gave the downbeat. The sixteenth notes were flying all over the place. Brass was playing, singing with the woodwinds and punctuated by the percussion section. All seemed to be in place, until the middle of the work. That is when I began to understand fear, if not violence!

Just before the love-making section in the music arrived, I had placed my left ear to the low timpani head and lightly tapped it while pedaling up to the required G. It felt right. Confident with the G, I tuned the upper D. I waited a few more measures to make my entrance. When my time came, I stroked the timpani at a pianissimo dynamic, while placing my notes ever so delicately with the pizzicato of the contrabasses. When I lifted my head to make eye contact with the maestro, I could see instantly that he was not happy. It seemed my ears were really not up to a satisfactory level, and certainly not a Comissiona level.

He stopped the orchestra and asked to hear my perfect fifths, which according to him were not so perfect. I played them as written, both together as double stops. Shaking his head from left to right in a very slow pace, he asked me to play them one at a time, starting with the G. I stroked the head at a mezzo forte level. Before the sound could actually make it to his ears, he was already shaking his head again in disapproval. "Your G is flat. Fix it, and do it quickly; you are wasting my time." I did my best to correct the pitch but was having a very difficult time hearing. The G sounded correct, so I wasn't sure how flat it actually was. The more I tried, the more I tensed up; the more I tensed up, the less I could hear. He began to shout louder, just about yelling, insisting I tune correctly.

By this time, I was humiliated, intimidated, and extremely nervous. There was almost nothing more I could do but look at him with an empty glance. He started again, "You obviously cannot hear the G, so tune the D first. Do it now and do it fast—you are wasting my time." At this point there was no way I could tune the two notes to a perfect unison, never mind a fifth. I simply fell apart.

In reality, he was correct to show his disapproval with my inability to tune properly. I was at fault, but he rode me like a cowboy attempting to set a new rodeo record! Why did he ride me so hard? Was it for personal satisfaction on his part? Did he think I was an awful musician? Or did he feel I had potential and wanted to foster my abilities on the spot? To this day, I don't know.

Nearly fourteen years had passed before our working relationship took form again in November of 1999 with the Holst. In 1999, when Comissiona was secured as guest conductor for a week with the New Jersey Symphony Orchestra, I was shaking at the mere thought of him directing me again in this, my professional work setting. Can you imagine how I felt when he set foot on the stage, stepped up to the podium, and took up his baton? Words cannot fully describe all the memories flooding back from *Don Juan*. There I was, playing with an orchestra that I had always dreamed of performing with, staring at the cold, lifeless eyes of the demon himself. In a word, fear.

Ironically, after the rehearsal concluded and I was making my way out of the building, the fiend and I bumped into each other in the hallway. As he lifted his tilted head and our eyes met, it seemed he remembered me. But this time, he remembered me from the rehearsal just performed. He commented on how wonderful the percussion section had sounded earlier that day.

CHAPTER 14

Ray

Only those in search of the truth can acquire true happiness.

—The author

June 23, 2003, 5:01 a.m., San Antonio, Texas:

I was in the airport waiting for my 6:00 a.m. flight. I had one goal in mind for my short stay in Texas: to visit my dear old pen pal, Ray Benjamin, and his wife, Margie, in Kerrville. For years I had been threatening Ray that I was going to make the journey to Kerrville for a face-to-face meeting. Since the first mention of the possibility, seven long years had passed. When I finally pulled the proverbial trigger and purchased my airline ticket, I began to be consumed with high emotions. My mind raced with both excitement and trepidation. I was to actually meet the person behind all the letters. Was he really like I imagined him to be? Was he as nice, caring, thoughtful, pleasant, and ambitious as his letters portrayed him to be? We were about to cross the line between fantasy and reality, and I was a bit taken aback by the thought. Perhaps I'd built it all up too much in my mind. Perhaps I was in for a real let-down and would never really recover from such a meeting. I had begun to build up this long overdue trip into absolute panic. I was questioning my every move, thought, and motive. In retrospect, these concerns couldn't be further from the truth. Now that I have actually made the journey, I was foolish for worrying in any way.

When I finally came to the decision to purchase an airline ticket, I knew I was going, and there was no turning back. Fifteen days prior to my departure date, I went online to seek out the best price for my airline ticket. After searching the net for endless hours (this was before I knew of such wonderful search engines), I came across a travel agent in Houston, Texas. I called the number indicated on the website, checked on my travel parameters, and purchased a round-trip ticket for $395. I was set to depart on June 21 at 6:00 a.m. from Newark International Airport, and I'd return on June 23, also departing at 6:00 a.m., from San Antonio. Once the ticket was secured, I reserved a small (*very* small, as I would soon find out) car to make the journey from San Antonio to Kerrville. Kerrville was about sixty-five miles northwest of the city. The price of the rental car came in at a comfortable forty-six dollars, which included unlimited mileage. Now, where to stay? I have traveled pretty extensively in my years, and one thing I have learned the hard way is that when it comes to accommodations, don't be cheap. I wanted to stay at a really nice hotel in the center of town, a location close to the Alamo and all the other attractions that the city had to offer. As fate would have it, a friend of mine who was touring with musical AIDA just happened to be in San Antonio during the same period. We had been staying in touch over the months of his busy tour, checking in from time to time. Through his affiliation with Disney (the touring company of AIDA), he was able to secure a deluxe room for me (which had two bathrooms and an extra-large refrigerator) for the low price of $58 per night—the normal "tourist" rate was $189 per night. This was the beautiful St. Anthony Hotel, located just a few short blocks from the Alamo. It was a perfect location, not too far from the airport. I was thrilled to have been able to score some points in my *less expense* column. Naturally, I accepted the fantastic deal on a great hotel and location. Everything was falling into place nicely.

In preparation of the historic meeting, I spent the next two weeks digging out all my old letters and pictures, sent to and received from Ray over the years. I couldn't decide if I should bring them with me or leave them home. Ultimately, I decided on leaving the letters home for safekeeping. I would later discover that Ray had copies of every correspondence that left New Jersey. While sifting through the letters, once again I was able to witness the development of this long-distance relationship. Tucked in the file with all the letters were countless photographs that carefully documented Ray and Margie's home, hobbies, family, and vast travels in their RV. Still sifting through the photographs, I noticed that some years back, Ray began collecting vintage diecast model cars. He began collecting cars after selling off much of his coveted vintage snare drum collection. After giving it some thought, I decided that a diecast 1950 model Chevy should put a smile on his face. A new quest has begun. I searched the Internet until I found exactly what I was looking for and made the purchase.

I was looking for some other offerings in addition to the newly acquired Chevy—something for Margie. I came across a delicately sculpted piece of crystal that housed the New York City Skyline in a three-dimensional setting. This seemed to be so appropriate for Margie. She had been tucked away in the middle of our great country for many years; I thought it would be nice to bring a little piece of the East Coast to her. After securing these two small gifts, I began to think it wasn't enough. I should bring them something more. I began sifting through our photographic exchanges over the years, and I put together a portfolio of my own; it was hundreds of pictures deep. I included all my favorite pictures of Ray and Margie's travels, vacations, tennis matches, and concert pictures, along with some pictures from my personal travels we had shared in the past. I really wanted to bring with me a very personal touch.

I still needed to bring another gift, something more to offer. I found myself going online to seek out all the companies that would deliver a gourmet basket to Kerrville. I was looking for jellies, fruits, pastries, breads, cheeses, and anything else that tickled my taste buds. After a thorough search, I came up with a few choices. However, the cost of delivery was more than the basket itself! Can you imagine that? It was amazing to me that companies would charge such an exorbitant fee for delivering their own products. In addition to the cost of the basket itself, the added cost of shipping perishables dróve the price up twenty-nine dollars more. To add insult to injury, none of these companies would deliver on a weekend, when I would arrive. When all was finally said and done, I decided to find some additional gifts in Kerrville upon my arrival. I felt I was set: the gifts were planned out, and the air, car, and hotel all arranged. All I needed to do was to wait for June 21 to roll around and then get on the plane.

With only a few more days to go, I began to think of what I was about to do, and why. The thought passed through my head that I was going to the same state where my father was living, and I was going to see a man who was probably around his age. But that thought came and went quickly. I was not going to see my father while visiting Texas. Instead, I was visiting a man who was *father-like* to me, in more ways than I ever imagined. Over the years, especially the past few, we had shared more than vintage drums and diecast cars. Without effort or even provocation, we had settled into some very personal exchanges. Our letters, although personal in nature, never made me feel uncomfortable. On the contrary, I felt extremely comfortable sharing some of my deepest thoughts and beliefs with a man I had never met.

For such a short stay, I wasn't planning on checking any luggage. Instead, I would just pack my well-weathered, overnight carry-on bag. After years of travel, I have been able to manage my life with every miniature item one can imagine. From an alarm clock to toothpaste, toothbrush, and deodorant, miniatures have indeed served me well. It was June 20, and my only chore for the day was to pack the miniature Chevy, the small gift for Margie, pictures, and a change of clothes into my compact carry-on. With that done, I had nothing left to do but wait for the appointed hour to leave for the airport. I went to bed early in anticipation of my early departure, but sleep didn't come easily. I tossed and turned for what felt like hours. In less than thirty-six hours I would be in Kerrville, meeting the man behind all those letters. At some point I finally fell asleep. My alarm was set to go off at 4:00 a.m., but I woke up out of a very sound sleep at 3:40. I glanced at the clock that sat on the far side of the bureau and thought it would be better to get up now than to let the alarm go off. I headed for the kitchen, switched on the already-prepared coffee pot, and waited until I heard the first sounds of percolation. Down I went to my studio (located in the basement of my home), where I took a very brief and cold shower and morning nature break. I was finished in minutes and had enough time to check my e-mail, feed the cat, and empty the dishwasher from the night before. My sister-in-law Diane had a moonlighting job that allowed her to create her own hours. On

Saturdays she normally arrived at work by six in the morning, and she worked though her shift without break. When I mentioned to her about my pending trip and the hour I needed to arrive at the airport, without hesitation she offered to take me. She was one fantastic sister-in-law!

Sure enough, at 4:30 a.m. Diane arrived at my house. Careful not to honk the horn at that hour, she waited in the driveway with her headlights peeking through the picture window. I looked out through the plants and shot a thumbs-up to her. I grabbed my bag and pulled the door tightly closed after setting the ever-reliable security system. The ride to the airport was uneventful, with the exception of my thanks for the ride, over and over again. Once at the airport, I kissed her on the cheek and headed off. At that moment it really hit me hard: I was really getting on a plane to Texas.

I had a connecting flight that first stopped at the Dallas–Ft. Worth Airport with a thirty-five minute layover and a change of aircraft. We disembarked the flight, and I saw the next departure gate just a few feet away. With a few minutes to spare, I decided to go outside and smell the Texas air. It was about 8:15 a.m. local time when I set foot for the first time on Texas soil. As the automatic doors of the *Salid* opened, I was hit with a blast of horribly humid eighty-six-degree air! It was only eight in the morning—what the heck was it going to be like at noon, or worse yet by 4:00 p.m.? The entire two days I spent in Texas, the temperature never went below seventy-nine degrees but never above 105, so I guess I shouldn't complain. I am told that the summers can get really hot, and this was actually not so bad.

After arriving at the San Antonio Airport, I proceeded to the rental car location, picked up my car, and started making my way to Route 281 south, in the direction of the St. Anthony Hotel in downtown San Antonio. Despite the detour signs, I found the hotel. I pulled into the valet parking area and handed my keys to the waiting attendant. I had arrived before check-in time but was accommodated as nicely as one can imagine. Upon entering my room, I noticed that it was spacious and lit with plenty of natural light. There were fruits, sodas, juices, and water, all complimentary, waiting for me in my room.

After unpacking the few items I'd brought with me, I placed a call to

Stan, my friend who was touring with AIDA. I was extremely weary from my sleepless night and morning travels, coupled with the now ninety-three-degree, moisture-soaked air. I let Stan know that I had arrived and was going to seek out some brunch. The hotel was located just a few blocks from the famous Riverfront Walk, which meant that a cup of coffee was only minutes away. With coffee in hand, I headed over to my choice of nearly fifty restaurants on the lower level of the walkway. Within a few minutes, a grilled chicken salad was sitting in front of me, and a few minutes after that, the plate was as clean as a whistle. I had been up for nearly ten hours without eating, and I was hungry! After lunch, I met up with Stan and headed over to the theater, where he would be playing his 2:00 p.m. matinee. I walked into the orchestra pit and checked out a fantastically elaborate percussion setup. I decided I would hang around in the pit for at least the first half of the show. By intermission time, I was ready to drop; I needed to put my head down on a soft pillow and close my eyes for a while. Stan and I made some plans to catch up later in the day.

While walking back to St. Anthony's Hotel via Broadway and Houston, I found myself getting dizzy from exhaustion and the thick, wet air. As soon as I reached my room, I turned on the shower and jumped under the cutting razors of the cool water. The chilly, clean water felt as if someone had given me a shot of adrenalin—how refreshing! Regardless of my newfound strength, I plopped my travel-weary body onto the bed. My plan was to sleep for an hour and then get up and walk to the area of the Alamo. As I lay down, I closed my eyes and thought about my big day, which was yet to come. The thought of my visit to Kerrville was so exciting to me that I was unable to even think of napping. With that, I got up, got dressed, locked room 733, and headed back out into the sultry air toward the Alamo.

During my walk around the Alamo area, I noticed that every block I walked up and down led me to more souvenir shops and crowded streets. I was astounded by the glut of vacationers, and then it dawned on me: it was a Saturday in June—what should I expect? I walked around for several hours until my cell phone rang. It was Stan; his show was over, and he was free for dinner. Once we met up, we took a walk back down to the River Walk and found a wonderful restaurant for dinner, The

Republic of Texas Restaurant and Night Club. Once seated, we talked some more about life on the road (Stan had been touring now for twenty-eight months) and general chitchat. Dinner was exceptionally good. It included a very spicy sopa de tortilla, along with el pollo rojo (an enchilada in red sauce with Monterrey jack cheese, served with Spanish rice and refried beans). After dinner, I ordered a homemade apple crisp along with an espresso. I figured the el pollo rojo, as well as the rest, was well deserved after the day I'd had.

Exhausted and stuffed, I returned to my hotel room; but this time my only mission was to get some sleep. It was only about 9:15 in the evening, but I didn't care—I was done. I got undressed, jumped back into the shower to wash off the city grime, and found myself back in bed by 9:30. Within minutes, I was enjoying a soft, goose-down pillow beneath my head, a soft but warm quilt atop my body, and the air-conditioning set on a cool sixty-three degrees.

June 22, Sunday: The Day We Met

My plan was to leave San Antonio at10:00 a.m. and drive to Kerrville, arriving by 11:30. I figured an hour and a half should be enough time for me to get there, get lost, and then get back on track. I woke up at 6:30 a.m. after a wonderful night's sleep (which was rare for me when I was not in my own bed). After showering, I went downstairs to the breakfast area and once again enjoyed exceptionally good service. The breakfast was served home-style and included juices, coffee, eggs, or freshly prepared omelets of choice, as well as breakfast meats, pancakes, waffles, French toast, and all the fixings one could imagine. I enjoyed a Texas-size breakfast in preparation of the day that was before me.

After my early breakfast, I went back to my room, where I did some writing, forcing myself not to leave too early for Kerrville. I wrote for about two hours before powering down my laptop. After standing up, stretching my legs, and twisting my torso from side to side, I began to feel the circulation enter my sedentary body. I gathered my gifts together for a slightly earlier departure and headed to the elevator. By 9:45 I was at the valet parking, retrieving my car from storage. The radio stated, "It's eighty-eight degrees, and the forecast is calling for temperatures to reach the low hundreds." I didn't need a weatherman to tell me that it has hotter than hell outside!

Off I went. I was terribly excited, and as the miles clicked away on my odometer, I grew more and more anxious. But this time it was an anxiety of great feelings. I turned on the radio and found, sandwiched between the country music stations, a classical station playing music of the Baroque period. (I later learned it was National Public Radio.) The time passed by quickly on this somewhat deserted Sunday morning highway.

And then there it was, directly in front of me: a sign that said "TX-16 S number 508." Kerrville was the next exit. As I took the exit and made my first left onto Route 16, I began to imagine what it must be like to live in Kerrville. For starters, Kerrville was in the mountainous region of Texas, and that helped bring in cooler weather. I learned from a local news station that Kerrville was a breezy ninety-four degrees upon my arrival.

I passed stores, restaurants, and shopping malls as I followed Route 16 for the three-plus miles my trusty map instructed. When I passed the Kerrville State Hospital, I knew I was close, because Ray had mentioned in his last letter to me that the hospital was only five minutes from his home.

I looked for Rio Robles Drive and then took a left and an immediate right onto Chapel Drive. I was now just a few blocks away and was jumping out of my skin with excitement. I knew I would recognize the house, because I had pictures sent to me some years earlier. I know there was an extension built a few years back because I had those photographs as well.

Looking at the house numbers I saw 4 and then 6; only a few more houses to go. There was 12 and finally 18. That didn't look like the house I remembered from the pictures, but it had to be. I was at the right address on the right day in the right city and state. That must be it! I pulled up in front of the house, noticing a white 1999 Ford sitting in the driveway. As I walked up to the front door, I saw through the window what appeared to be a computer. I knew Ray did not own a computer, so I figured I was at the wrong house. I pressed the doorbell and waited. My heart was no longer pumping as rapidly as it had been a few moments earlier.

Now I was truly perplexed and somewhat deflated. I glanced at my watch, and it was 11:30 a.m. on the nose, the time we had agreed to our gathering. After no one answered the door, I got in my car and drove back up the road, stopping to ask a neighbor if I was in the right place. They told me, "Absolutely, just head down to eighteen." Ultimately, I picked up my cell phone and dialed Ray's number.

"Hello?" Ray answered.

"Ray, where the heck are you?" I asked.

"Well, I am here, where are you?" he responded. I explained my state of affairs, and he chuckled and asked me to head down Chapel Drive once again. This time, Ray was standing outside his doorway.

We greeted each other without any nervousness whatsoever. I was so comforted to see him and find him that all the fears I had concerning our little get-together turned into distant memories. Ray later explained that the doorbell had a mind of its own and would sometimes get confused with a neighbor's bell.

After a firm handshake and a quick gaze into each other's eyes, I told Ray that I needed to get some things out of the car. While walking back, my heart began to race again; not from the unknown but from an excitement that might come but once in a lifetime. I went back to the car to collect the parcels that had made the journey with me, as well as what I had gathered in Kerrville upon my arrival. I gathered them up and walked into his home—Ray and Margie's home. Ray's lovely wife, Margie, allowed me without hesitation to kiss her on her cheek, and she greeted me warmly. I offered her the plant and flowers I had purchased in Kerrville, and she accepted them with blushing cheeks.

I began to look around their home; everything looked exactly as I had pictured it. Everything looked just like the photos we had shared in past correspondences. I didn't know what to do first. Should we talk, should I look around, or should I offer the other gifts I had brought? No idea. Ray quickly took over; I am sure he sensed my nervousness. His first remarks included his absolute delight that I had made the trip. (Later, Margie shared with me that Ray had been fidgeting all week in anticipation of my visit. Ray even called me just a few days before my departure to see if I was still coming—for some reason he really wasn't sure or believed it to be so.)

There was music playing in the house: nice, cool jazz, not too loud and not too soft. As I allowed my eyes to pan around the room, I noticed sitting on top of the music center were a sea of memoires reflected in family photographs; more insight to the Benjamin's became apparent. Just to the left of the music center was the famous addition that was built some years back. Ah, this was what I remembered from the photographs! From some pictures Ray had sent to me years prior to my visit, I imagined that the addition, (a large, glassed-in porch) was on the front of the house, not the side. Furthermore, Ray and Margie had painted the house, thus confusing me more when I first arrived. I commented that it was a nasty trick to play on their friend from New Jersey, and we all laughed.

My mind began to race as I wanted to say everything I had prepared for weeks in one long sentence, but once again Ray rescued me from my inarticulate ways. He invited me into what I would call his inner sanctum. This room, which sat at the front of the house, was flooded with sunlight. I found it to be a cheerful place, and we spent the next portion of our visit there. This room once held an enormous collection of vintage snare drums and memorabilia from days gone by. The room still housed many snare drums—by my recollection, ten in all. As we walked into the room, my eyes panned back and forth several times, unable to focus on all the wonderful items, and not only the fantastic pieces of history that sat high above his desk on shelving units designed by the master himself, but collections of letters, stock portfolios, and file cabinets. There was also his collection of diecast vintage model cars.

When I looked at the cars, my heart nearly stopped beating. Why? Well, Ray had a vast collection of these model cars, which he had sent many photographs illustrating. From the looks of the photographs, I imagined that the cars were much larger than they actually were. I had purchased a 1:24 Chevy, whereas he had all 1:43 scale cars. I didn't fully understand what all those numbers meant two weeks ago. In my quest for a perfect gift, I had started to do some research on model cars, knowing that Ray had a huge collection. I took out all the pictures he had sent me, and looked for some model that was not pictured. I saw a 1950 Chevy that looked wonderful, so I placed my order. A few days later, the car arrived at my home from California. I opened it and examined the Chevy to see if there were any visible defects; everything looked fine. Then I took the photos out that Ray had sent some years earlier and compared the Chevy to the cars in the pictures. It appeared to be a perfect match, so I was thrilled with my impulse to snatch up this Chevy. Little did I know that the scale was way off the mark. It was at this point that I said to Ray that he needed to open up the other items I had brought with me.

I went inside, through the living room, and into the kitchen to retrieve the package I had brought with me. I handed it over to Ray so he could unwrap the offering. I was blushing partly because I loved to give gifts to friends, and partly because the size of the car was gargantuan compared to what I saw sitting before me. He unwrapped the gift, carefully opened the box, pulled the tissue paper back, and peered in. His blue eyes widened with excitement—or concern, I thought. But no, Ray was indeed an exceptional man; he never once alluded to the enormity of the car. On the contrary, he shared the offering with Margie, who smiled with appreciation and then took it over to the mantle on the fireplace. Sitting on top of the mantel was a 1:24 model of a trailer-hitched RV, full to scale, and a perfect reproduction (I am sure) of one once owned by this adorable couple. He placed the Chevy next to the RV and stated that it was a perfect mate for his RV. Regardless of the validity of the statement (which I believed to be true), Ray eased my mind and made me feel wonderful once again. All my anxieties were somewhere back on Highway 10, between San Antonio and Kerrville.

Back in the inner sanctum, sitting on Ray's desk were vintage drum books and catalogs that he had shared with me years earlier. To the left of the drum books were photographs I had once possessed, which traveled to Kerrville long before I had made my trip. I was so taken aback by the vision of *my* photographs; I was truly speechless. Like me, Ray still possessed these memories. Hanging on the wall, just to the left of the word processor (not computer) were plaques and acknowledgments of Ray's past. There was an honorary document from the musicians union declaring Ray a lifetime member, as well as a degree certifying

Ray as a graduate of geology. These were among the four carefully placed hangings that offered more insight into this pen pal of mine.

I found Ray to be a meticulous man, extremely organized and very thorough in his filing system. I was beginning to see how much we really had in common. Throughout the day, during lunch, and during a very pleasant scenic drive of Kerrville, we shared endless stories; there was never a lull in our conversation. After our lunch and sightseeing excursion, we returned back to 18 Chapel Drive to enjoy some strawberry and mint chocolate chip ice cream. Margie helped herself to two servings, first the strawberry followed by the mint chocolate chip. We sat down in the living room, which was quite comfortable and had a lived-in feeling; it made me feel very much at home. While eating ice cream and sharing more stories of work, family, and life in general, I discovered some very interesting facts about Mr. Benjamin on that fateful Sunday afternoon. Ray was a native of Canada who had settled in Texas back in 1967. He worked for the oil companies as a hands-on troubleshooter. His work took him to all corners of the world, which made for a very interesting thirty-plus-year career. I was truly taken aback by the stories of his travels and experiences.

It was approaching 4:00 p.m., and I was beginning to feel like I was overstaying my welcome. I didn't want to leave, but I didn't want to impose on Ray and Margie's hospitality beyond what I felt was right. At the stroke of four, I began to hear birds singing. I didn't think much of it, other than maybe I was hearing things, or was just tired. Although I tried to pick myself up and depart, a few more hours passed. During those few hours I would make comments like, "I should be going," or "I would like to get back to San Antonio before dark." I was waiting to see Ray's reaction, but he never reacted the way I expected. After my long visit, I thought that they were surely tired of entertaining me. On the contrary—if they were, they never showed it. Once again I began to hear birds singing, but this time caught a glimpse of the culprit. There was a clock next to the new addition of the house, just to the right of the double-glass doors. A bird would sing each hour that passed, with the tune of twelve different species. I felt better knowing that I wasn't losing my mind and had only one regret: I wish I could have stayed to hear all twelve birds sing.

It was now after 6:00 p.m., and I felt that the time had indeed come for me to take my leave. I could have stayed all night, no question, as I felt full acceptance from my dear friends in Kerrville. It was then that Ray took me back to the inner sanctum and began sharing with me more details of his life. When I first arrived, I had noticed tags on each of the ten or so drums. It was now that I was told that each tag had a name on it: the name of the person who would receive the instrument after Ray passed. Reality began to settle in. We spoke of Margie and her continuing battle with Alzheimer's disease, and the toll it had taken on him. We spoke about the process of aging, those who had passed on before us, and so much more. It was during this conversation that Ray repeatedly expressed his gratitude for my visit. He told me that I was an exceptional man with a big heart. I responded, "On the contrary, *you* are the exceptional man. I made the journey for you."

His next words will stick with me for the rest of my life. "You are like my adopted son, Jim." I returned the honest feeling that he was certainly an adopted father for me. Not wanting to cry in front of him, I turned the conversation to our next visit. I assured Ray that the time would come again, sooner rather than later.

As we walked out of the front room, we walked right by his journals, which went back nearly forty years. I found that amazing. He had kept a collection of journals, marking each day, each month, and each year for roughly forty years and counting. The journals were all placed in chronological order and sat upon a shelf that I remembered from pictures he had sent many years ago. I reached out, grabbed one toward the middle of the vast collection, and began to read. As I thumbed through his offering, I was careful not to intrude too deeply on his writings. I was impressed, to say the least. Such dedication to any craft is surely worth mentioning. Additionally, I was envious on some level, but in the same thought I made the connection of my own writings, which Ray had helped to inspire. So we had come full circle—writings, pictures, gifts, love, feelings, and a plethora of other emotions.

Before we said our good-byes, we took the opportunity to mark the day with a photo op; I thought it was fitting. First, Margie and I stood in front of the fireplace, my left hand delicately placed on her left shoulder. With one simple click, the memory was captured. Then Margie took a photograph of Ray and me in the same location. Our arms crisscrossed each other's backs, and as the camera made its familiar sound, our hands, which were on top of each other's opposite shoulder, squeezed tightly. With that squeeze, I held back my tears yet again. The final shot of the afternoon was a picture I asked if I might take, of both Ray and Margie. Ray was only happy to comply, but he asked that I make sure I get the 1950 Chevy in the picture. The Chevy was sitting next to the RV on top of the fireplace. I was sure to get it in the viewfinder.

Before I left Ray and Margie, they gave me a few gifts. The gifts that Ray had so thoughtfully picked out for me were exceptionally special. A verbal history of drummer Ray Tough (now documented in writing), along with a pair of his actual wire brushes, and a *Down Beat Magazine* dated December 1938. The magazine was littered with Tough's name throughout. He also presented me with a vintage drum key from the twenties, a wonderful addition to my growing collection. All of these gifts would be cherished and kept for the remainder of my days.

At nearly 9:00 p.m., I pulled slowly out of 18 Chapel Drive to begin my drive back to San Antonio. The sixty-five-mile drive flew by in what felt like ten minutes. I drove the entire way without any radio; I was lost in my thoughts about what had just taken place. I wondered when I would get back down to Kerrville, and I felt I had been blessed a million times over for meeting a couple like the Benjamins. My little contribution to their lives and their large one to mine would remain emblazoned in my memory for a long time to come.

I am still unsure about the exact reason for my visit. Was it selfishly for me? Was I looking for the answer to unasked questions? If so, what would those questions be? For now, all I know is, I spent the best nine hours of my life in Kerrville on a hot summer day in June.

CHAPTER 15

The Next Chapter

Journal Entry: October 27, 2003

It was five months ago that I first heard that the personnel manager of the New Jersey Symphony Orchestra was retiring. I have to admit, I began to imagine myself in his shoes—or better yet, his job. Weeks had passed since the rumor had circulated, and the thought of becoming the next personnel manager began to fade away. It was not until a number of colleagues approached me during a rehearsal break and said, "Jim, you will take Charlie's job, won't you? I think you would be great." And, "I am going to talk to management and voice my opinion." This was the tone for the next two weeks straight, and I must admit, while I was mulling over the idea of having this prominent job, I was well aware of the enormous responsibilities that accompanied such a position.

As the buzz continued to build, I decided to ask the man himself. I walked over to Charlie and asked if I could have a word with him at a suitable time. Much to my shock, he accepted me that very day. Without sufficient time to prepare a proper statement or formulate clear and cohesive thoughts, I agreed to see him after the morning rehearsal concluded. We met in his private room on the second floor of the NJPAC. Charlie motioned for me to take a seat, and I did with great trepidation. I awkwardly began to express some thoughts, but nothing was making any sense. After running out of ideas on how I should put together my question, I simply asked him why he thought I had asked to see him.

He responded with a shrug of his shoulders. "I have no idea." As his shoulders dropped fully, he asked me to continue.

Still at a loss for words, I began telling him that I had not spoken to anyone, but people were approaching me. "They were dropping statements about your imminent retirement."

He chuckled and said, "That's it?" Then something happened that I never expected—not before, not then, and not even now! Charlie began to talk to me candidly about the job, citing several examples along the way. This conversation lasted well over an hour. I think in the four years I spent at the symphony on a regular basis, I had a total of thirty minutes' worth of conversation with him before this.

Along with various stories of music directors, management, musicians, and union issues, he reminded me that with my business (Arts Alive International, Inc.), I was my own boss. I would later do a lot of reflecting on this very important point. As the conversation wound down, he gave me his blessing and wished me good luck with the process. He told me that he was going to resign as soon as he remembered how to spell *resignation*. Typical Charlie.

June rolled in, and there was still no word on Charlie's intended departure. However, my fantasizing was increasing, imagining what my new role would be like. I began to work daily on the computer, formulating questions that may be asked on an interview, searching all information and taking notes.

Sometime in the middle of June, I received an e-mail from Charlie. I was almost too excited to open it. Was this the e-mail I had been waiting for, for months now? When I opened it, I began to read quickly. It contained an offer to play the pops series, along with the schedule. I was actually upset that I was offered work and that it was not about the job! Of course, I accepted the work. It was during this period that the buzz in the orchestra began to flare up again.

I had been planning an August trip to London to visit my nephew, who was bettering his academic career through his studies at Cambridge. I kept putting off my plans, not booking hotels or an airline ticket, in the hopes that the magical announcement and subsequent interview would take place. During a long discussion during the pops series, Charlie had confided in me that he planned to retire on September 1, as it would be his fifteenth anniversary as personnel manager, and it would also coincide with his fifty-fifth birthday. He had spent fifteen years working as personnel manager and wanted out—did he know something that I did not?

Stagehands were also instrumental in keeping me up to date with developments, because they were around management daily and had their finger on the inner pulse of the organization. My friend, a stagehand, would report to me whenever we would get together. On July 5, the symphony played an outdoor concert in Montclair; it was at this concert that a friend told me he had overheard the production manager say that I was the guy for the job. I did not want to believe him, but I could not help but be excited. I even considered canceling my pending Cambridge trip. There was no way I was going to miss the opportunity of a possible interview with the powers that be. I was hopeful, to say the least. I also learned that the general manager was aware of the many European trips I had run in the past, which was a highly positive point. Things were lining up for me. I felt it, I believed it, I wanted it. I *really* wanted it, and I felt it was within my grasp.

The news of Charlie submitting his retirement papers came from more the ten people. Calls and e-mails alerted me to his ultimate decision and submission of the all-important resignation letter. That very day, I dropped off my well-crafted letter of intent to the offices of the symphony. I had carefully chosen every word. I did my best not to sound overeager while portraying my confidence in being qualified for the position.

By July 25 I still had not heard of any official interview. That led me to the following decision (after fighting bitterly with my brother over this issue): I was getting on the next plane to London. I needed a break. If the symphony called, I would be able to retrieve my messages from London and jump back to New Jersey in a day's notice. In less than thirty-six hours, I was in London and staying at the beautiful St. Ermin's Hotel on 2 Caxton Street. The hotel was just around the corner from Scotland Yard and St. James Park.

London came and went. No call came, no letter, no nothing. My emotions were going through extreme highs and lows in anticipation, and I wondered whether the process (which actually never began) was getting to me, or whether I getting to myself. My brother's angry words began to ring loudly in my ears. "Don't think about the job or interview until *they* give you something to think about!" Of course he was correct, but at that time, I was blind with desire.

I received another e-mail from Charlie somewhere in the second week of August, requesting my services at the PNC Arts Center for a concert of opera favorites a few weeks away, I accepted. It was at this series that I was informed that there had been a hold placed on the search for a personnel manager until after Labor Day. Toward the end of August, I received another e-mail from Charlie requesting my services for the Symphony Gala concert, which took place at the beginning of September. *What the heck is going on?* I was on an emotional roller coaster. *What are they waiting for? He is out on September 1, right?*

At the same time all this was taking place, I had rekindled a relationship with a dear friend and mentor, the president of the Mannes College of Music, Chuck Kaufman. I shared with him the past months' events and concerns. As I should have expected, in his own inevitable way Chuck began to pave the way for my return to sanity. I was grateful that he was able to bring some calm back into the process, as I had been at wits' end for several weeks.

I would learn a number of things in the days to come. Charlie was staying on indefinitely, and the symphony was going through very difficult contract negotiations. Negotiations were a large contributor to the process being slowed down, but more important, the symphony was putting the final touches on a much higher position than the orchestra personnel manager. They were finalizing the top position in the organization. The appointment of their new music director, Neeme Järvi, was announced a few weeks later.

Good things come to those who wait. As fate would have it, in October I had the interview for the position, and I was ultimately offered the job. All the waiting, the months of uncertainty and anxiety, family arguments, a trip to London, and a lot of performances—those were forgotten in a flash. I accepted the position of orchestra personnel manager of the New Jersey Symphony Orchestra on the twenty-fourth of the month, which happened to coincide with my fortieth birthday. This was one present on a milestone birthday that I would never forget.

CHAPTER 16

AAI is born

In 1994 I began traveling overseas to perform with various United States–based orchestras and chamber ensembles. I was happy to be employed, traveling the world, and visiting countries I may never have considered as a tourist. From Western Europe to the Eastern bloc, from Iceland through Bulgaria and Romania, each trip carried new experiences with a realization of dreams and financial rewards. Of course, all this fun was accompanied by various problems and mishaps.

A few years earlier, I was asked to manage a small orchestra based in New Jersey. Before I accepted this position, I made sure that there would be no conflicts of interest. I would accept the position, as long as I would be able to continue performing as principal timpanist, while managing the affairs of the orchestra membership. I was assured that was precisely what management desired. They felt that by combining the two positions, they would gain a well-rounded contractor, one who was in the thick of it with the musicians but amendable with their superiors. Within a few months, we mutually found things were running smoothly, and both factions felt comfortable with me in my new management role.

The following season, we performed some concerts as a joint effort with various New Jersey–based choruses. It was then that a wonderful thing happened. When the music directors of the choruses heard "my" orchestra, they would hire me on the spot to put together an ensemble for their chorus concerts in the months to come! This phenomenon took place time after time, until one day I was managing five local choruses. As my reputation grew, other regional orchestras made the same offer as the original; to manage the affairs of their organization. In some cases, the new groups offered me a performing position, to help entice me to accept the management position. In a short amount of time, I had four more groups under my belt.

I was feeling good, and I was learning and beginning to understand the music business more intimately. I started to develop good people skills, because a large part of my job was to serve the musicians and their needs. Providing a professional atmosphere for people to accomplish the same goal was my primary concern. I maintained the idea that if a good working environment is provided, musicians and the music director should excel in the art of making music.

In 1996 I was on a two-week concert tour in Central Europe with a Washington DC–based chamber orchestra. As we were crossing the Slovak Republic and Austria frontier, I watched with my own eyes the logistics of what appeared to be carefully executed plans for a successful tour fall apart. The Austrian Police (Bundespolizei) questioned the tour guide as to why we were crossing the border. The poor guide, who was just doing her job, slowly sank into her worn-out bus seat, only to begin welling up with tears. In less than five minutes, the guide simply broke down, unable to continue with the barbarian affront to civilization. The bus driver jumped into the conversation to offer help; he began to explain that the orchestra was from the United States and was on tour in Central Europe. We were going just thirty minutes over the border to Vienna. The driver offered further information as to the location of the concert, which was scheduled for later the same evening. The more the driver spoke, the worse the situation became. This went on for more than an hour before the Bundespolizei ordered everyone off the bus. Once off the bus, all passports were collected, and they began the painstaking task of documenting everyone's information—by hand! This took several hours to accomplish, which pushed our concert start time to the brink of no return.

I sat quietly observing the events that had unfolded in front of my eyes, still in disbelief. How could something like this happen? How could we be detained for three and a half hours? I later learned that the carnet form was not filled out properly; this coupled with years of disdain between the Slovaks and Austrians had triggered the entire episode. A carnet form is an international customs and export-import document that houses all instruments traveling to and from a country. For each entrance and exit, the form must be stamped with approval. For starters, our form was carelessly filled out, neglecting to list each and every musical item with us. Where our tour organizer listed a Cooper violin, they did not list the bow that was needed to play the violin. The Austrians did not agree that the violin and bow counted as one instrument and thought (or so they said) we were going to sell all the items left off the carnet form on the black market while in Vienna.

I couldn't believe my ears, not only for the naivety of the border guards, but for the unthinkable omission of the US-based tour company. If they were in the business of sending orchestras all over the world to perform, they should know the protocol inside and out.

It was during these few hours of absolutely wasted time that my disbelief turned into understanding; a light bulb went off over my head. I began to see how I could merge music performance with the music business through my own booking company. We too could tour worldwide, and I could see to it that nothing horrible like this would ever happen again.

It was now July 3, 1996, in Vienna, Austria. While standing high above Stephansplatz in Vienna, a thought came to the forefront of my mind. Are all music promoters completely incompetent? It didn't seem so difficult to conceptualize success, detail, and preparation, and then act on it. This thought was magnified due to several factors that impacted our current performance tour. Crossing the border was at the top of the screw-up list, but it was a very long list.

During the flight home and after my arrival, I couldn't shake the idea that formed while in Europe. There was only one thing to do: do well what others were doing poorly. The question was, how? I knew there was a lot I needed to learn about putting a tour together—all the pitfalls and problems, never mind finding a good organizer overseas, which was no easy feat. Fortunately, by then I had been traveling pretty extensively, and had met an individual who knew a great deal about touring, travel, and the business of concert promotion. Şölen and I had begun our relationship several years before my revelation. I called on him for advice, and later we would partner on various events and tours throughout the world. Feeling armed with newfound knowledge and a source who was willing to work with me, I pushed forward. I decided the time was right; it was time to make my move.

By the end of 1997, Arts Alive International was born. Soon after conception, Arts Alive was incorporated for protection; we were now AAI Inc. Within a few weeks, we secured a toll-free number (888.900. ARTS), printed stationery, and created a website. It wasn't long after that when Uncle Sam began to receive quarterly deposits from AAI's coffers. With continued support from Şölen, we began partnering on several overseas ventures. All were met with complete success, and we had a following of repeat customers. This was an incredible period to be traveling. The US dollar was booming, and costs overseas were at a minimum. We rode the gravy train of European travel for many happy years, making plenty of money for both of us.

Another reason for forming AAI was to create a viable contracting company in the New York and New Jersey area. AAI offered what other companies couldn't: a one-stop, complete production company. AAI was a company that would prepare every aspect of a performance, no matter how small or large, to perfection. We paid exceptional care to detail. AAI would arrange everything from rehearsal and performance venues, music purchase, securing all personnel and payroll. AAI was able to pick up each of the choruses I had been working with previously as my first clients.

Before creating AAI, clients were writing checks to me, James Neglia. These funds would be used to pay those I hired on behalf of their organization. However, many of my clients, old and new, felt a bit uncomfortable writing a twenty-five-thousand-dollar check to an individual. People found it more palatable to write a check to a company, and one which had liability insurance to boot. So be it. I hired an accountant and placed a lawyer on retainer to help with unforeseeable problems. I purchased the latest version of QuickBooks, opened an account at PaineWebber, had company checks made up, and began making deposits.

It was my brother John's idea to come up with the little dancing *As* for the Arts Alive logo. I loved it and quickly incorporated the logo on my checks, website, and letterhead. He felt the dancing *As* reflected a calm, smooth operation.

In the beginning, I was spending more time on the phone, balancing the company checkbook, and writing contracts than I was practicing and performing. It was a very tricky transition period, and I had difficulties balancing my old life as an artist and my new life as a businessman. After the first year passed, I gained a better business perspective and was able to get my work done in less time; this helped my time management and offered more time in the practice room. My determination was at an all-time high, and as I found my footing with Arts Alive, performing became easier and less strained. Everything was falling into place nicely.

Fearing some irreparable issue somewhere down the road would ensue, I decided that before getting screwed in ways I haven't even imagined, I would have my lawyer draw up an iron-clad client contract. We came up with a contract that bound my employees to a particular event. My lawyer and my accountant suggested securing liability insurance immediately. Because I was booking events all over the world, the insurance company needed to create a specialized type of liability insurance. If I hired a musician to work at Carnegie Hall, and he broke his leg, *I* would get sued, not the concert hall. If someone was robbed in Helsinki, *I* was responsible. Liability insurance came in at the highest possible premium, but I paid the price to be protected from the elements waiting for me down the road.

Over the years, Arts Alive grew into my full-time job. I wasn't making enough money to bring in a full staff, but I did hire a secretary; her main tasks were to stay in touch with clients, answer emails and phone calls, run payroll, file contracts, and so on. In the meantime, I was driving all over New York, New Jersey, Connecticut, and Pennsylvania to meet with new clients. After an initial phone conversation, I had a good idea whether I needed to make a personal trip to solidify the deal. Most times not, but sometimes it was a must. The larger projects always called for at least one visit, and understandably so, because some of the contracts were two-week performance trips to Europe with an orchestra of eighty people.

AAI made more money in the first few years organizing concerts than I had made personally in the past ten of my career as a percussionist. Producing concerts and recording sessions all over the world proved to be a lucrative path. As the business grew, so did my frequent flyer miles. Projects in Central Europe were thriving; everyone and their uncle wanted to record in Prague or Bratislava. The dollar was incredibly strong, and we used it to our advantage. US-based companies would pay roughly twenty-five cents on the dollar for a project produced in Europe. The profit margin was enormous, and I was thrilled.

However, the profits didn't come without lots of hard work, determination, understanding, and a pinch of risk. Many times I would find myself flying from the United States with tens of thousands of dollars taped to my legs, chest, and waist to pay some organization in Europe. The greenback was king, and everyone wanted a piece of it, everyone wanted their fees in US dollars! AAI's payment would come in the form of a wire transfer, which would account for the other 75 percent of the budget not used. This would generally triple, if not quadruple, our initial project investment. This process took place time and time again, affording me my north Jersey home as well as one seaside at exit 63. To quote Dickens, "It was the best of times …"

CHAPTER 17

Joe Gould's Secret

Journal Entry: April 14, 1999

My friend Michael received a call from a large New York casting agency. Lisa enquired if he was available to play the vibraphone in a movie being shot in Brooklyn later that week. Mike informed Lisa that he did not play the vibes but knew someone who did. That someone was me. After a short conversation with Lisa, we came to an agreement on a fee for the rental and delivery of the vibraphone. The fee for performing was already set according to union rules. After I hung up, I realized that in my excitement, I had forgotten to ask her what piece of music I would be playing in this movie. I called back and asked the all-important question. She asked me if I knew the old jazz standard "Cherokee."

"Of course!" I said. The truth was, I'd never heard the tune before in my life. The movie shoot was just five days away, and I had never heard the music I was about to perform. I went to my file cabinet where I store music I rarely need. Thank goodness I had a copy of the *Real Jazz Standards*. I opened the book to the table of contents, and there it was, sandwiched among the 420 pages. I began to look at it, study it, and learn it. As I was playing through the tune, I suddenly realized that I really had no clear idea of how this would play out. Would I be playing just the melody, or the just chords, or both together?

My job would be to mime the tune in the movie while the tune was playing through a monitor. I started to think of every movie I had seen where I laughed at the actor trying to mime or fake a tune. They all

111

looked so ridiculous. I wasn't about to look ridiculous, too. I called Lisa once again and asked her if she would send me a tape of the music that I would be playing, so I would be 100 percent prepared. In order not to appear to be faking, I wanted to know what key and style the tune was to be performed in, because there are many interpretations—blues, bossa nova, and ballad. Which one would it be? I was told a practice tape would arrive via FedEx before noon the next day.

The next day at about 1:00 p.m., I placed another phone call to Lisa informing her that the tape never arrived. She told me that the movie company was having difficulties securing the rights to "Cherokee," and that I would not be performing it. Instead, I would be playing to warm-ups on tape. "Warm-ups? What do you mean, warm-ups?" She told me I would be playing the part of a jazz vibraphonist warming up before the evening gig. This was not good news. What was I going to do? I asked her if she could send over the warm-ups that were going to be used. She said that she would get them out as soon as she had them. A few days passed, and still no tape.

It was now one day before the taping. At about 10:00 a.m. I received a FedEx package from New York. I ripped open the sealed envelope, grabbing the tape with one hand while opening the tape player with the other. I placed the tape in the player and began to listen. My ears beheld the full story; on the tape, there was nothing but mindless music dribble. There was no rhyme or reason to it. No beat, no pattern, no timing, no nothing. I had no idea what I was going to do. I had no choice—listen again, and try to write it down. I sat down with manuscript paper and tried to write down in musical terms what I was hearing on the tape. It was impossible. I listened over and over again, but nothing I did or wrote seemed to work. I spent the next several hours trying to work it out. Finally, at about 4:00 I called Lisa and explained my dilemma. Ultimately, I asked her if it would be okay for me to play live in the movie. She explained to me that there were additional fees for live performance in a motion picture, and she needed to remain true to her budget. I told her that I would waive all additional fees, but I would feel more comfortable if I could perform what was in my own head and not on the tape. We agreed.

My call was for 6:45 the next morning in Brooklyn, at a local watering hole that had already been retro-fitted to look like a 1940s bar. I parked my car with forty-five minutes to spare, but I stayed in the driver's seat for a few minutes until I went over what I was going to play.

As I got out of my car, I saw people milling about close to the bar. About twenty yards away from the bar was a fantastic sight. The crew was set up for breakfast, and there was food everywhere. There was a chef outside, filling orders at that hour. I saw every type of Danish pastry, doughnut, and bagel I could imagine. There were a couple of dozen different flavored coffees, as well as flavored creams. It was amazing! I casually walked over to the breakfast buffet without appearing too eager. I hesitantly asked for an egg on a bagel and a large hazelnut coffee. The cook never lifted his eyes and simply filled my order. I was on the inside, and it felt great.

With bagel and coffee in hand, I figured I ought to check in somewhere, but where? I started walking around, keeping an eye out for people who looked like they knew what they were doing. I ran into a woman named Alexis, and she told me to sit tight and not get lost in the shuffle.

At 7:25 a.m. a woman named Julie approached. She walked around with an air of absolute certainty and confidence, like she ran the place. She asked me if I would bring my vibraphone into the bar, set it up, and head over to wardrobe. I went back to my car, unpacked the vibes, and wheeled them into the bar. I placed them close to a group of five tables just across from the bar itself; this was where my scene was to take place. My heart began to pump harder and faster. Some of the people who were working on the setup asked me if I would play them something, and naturally I did. I was just doodling on the instrument, feeling right at home, when all of a sudden Julie rushed in and made it clear that I was to go to wardrobe immediately.

Wardrobe was a few blocks away. Julie pointed me in the right direction, handed me a voucher, and sent me on my way. I arrived at a long row of trailers and began looking for number six. I located it, knocked on the door, and then entered. Alexis was there, waiting for me. She introduced me to the wardrobe people and also the barber. (Uh oh!) The first thing I did was get undressed. For the next fifteen minutes, every kind of suit imaginable found its way over the curtain. "Try this one on; let's see what you look like." The last one I tried on fit me like a glove. The suit, typical of the forties, was simple yet perfect. It was somewhat lavender with a silk, peach-colored shirt. I'd wear my own shoes. Next, Alexis sat me down in front of a circle of those mega-watt light bulbs, put her right hand on my left shoulder (was that a sympathetic gesture I was feeling?), and said, "Sorry, Jim, the mustache and beard have to go."

I almost died. "What?" I whined, "Please, not the mustache; it took me thirty-five years to grow it!" I also tried to convince her that a good, close trim on the beard would do the job. We compromised: mustache stayed, beard was gone.

While I was sitting in the wardrobe and makeup trailer, producer, director, and star of the film Stanley Tucci walked in and sat down next to me to begin the makeup process. Alexis made the introductions. There he was, Stanley Tucci! I found him to be warm and welcoming. He was about my height and build, yet I viewed him as a giant. He asked me if I'd had some breakfast. I told him I wasn't hungry. (If I would have eaten anything more, I certainly would have thrown up.) We chatted for a few minutes, small talk, and then I asked him why he chose the vibraphone as the solo instrument in his movie. He explained to me in depth about his love of jazz; his mother had bought a vibraphone for him many years ago. "The vibes are still in my apartment," he said.

I excused myself when Alexis asked me to follow her to the sound check. Tucci smiled and said, "I will see you in a little while." We walked over to the bar without conversation. I was nervous, but I knew I could play.

Enter Sam, a little guy, maybe an inch over five feet. He was the sound engineer. He asked me if I would play something for him so he could set the microphone level. We spent about thirty seconds doing our thing, and that was that. A few minutes later, Tucci walked in. The time had come, and with his characteristic half-smile, he looked at me and quietly said, "Here we go."

We ran through the scene a few times with the cameras rolling, but something always went wrong. On the third take, Tucci was playing with a pen while speaking to a friend. As he was twirling the pen, it exploded and ink flew everywhere. Tucci never flinched as three people ran up to him and wiped his hands. Moments later, we were once again ready to roll.

A distant voice yelled, "Rolling!" and then "Action!" I was on. I mean, "Action!" meant, "Jim, play now." I began a simple melody in C minor, a great blues key. As I was playing, the doodling started to sound like an actual tune. "Cut!" a very loud voice yelled. I thought another pen had exploded, but no, this time it was me. "Jim, you cannot play anything that sounds like a real tune—nothing. Understand?" Tucci looked over at me with that same half-smile and said, "Man, that's a hard task."

No kidding, I thought. "Okay, let's go."

Once again I was on. I heard, "Play now," and I did. Soon we were cooking. The scene began with the camera on my vibes, on the low end to my left. As I played, the camera panned out from my hands to my body, and finally over to the action at the tables. I continued playing through the three-minute scene. "Cut! Print that." That was it, over, finito.

"Really?" I said.

Stanley looked over to me with two thumbs up. "Great, Jim!"

People seemed to be so impressed with my little doodling on the vibes. Stanley asked me to play through the lunch break for the crew. He was so friendly, courteous, and un-imposing! Tucci asked the sound engineer for a playback of the scene. Within seconds, the scene was playing on a small monitor behind me. Stanley asked if I would be willing to doodle some more, for safety's sake. What was I going to say? This time he directed me for ten minutes. Now Tucci himself politely asked for silence; the room fell still. In a voice barely above a whisper, he said, "Roll audio, please." He looked me square in the eyes and said, "Play a lick, like ba-do-doda-da-di and repeat it three times, with a second off in between."

"Okay." I sensed his keen knowledge of the instrument, and what he wanted from me.

"Again, Jim, again." I nodded. "Now, from the top down, but short and softer." I nodded. "Now, a not-too-fancy lick that you can repeat over and over." I nodded. "Now, a really fast lick like, dagada-dagada-dagada-dagada." I continued to nod and give him whatever he wanted.

Finally, he looked at me and said, "Great, we have it." That was it, really.

115

It was all over, completely. The forty or so people on the set broke into spontaneous applause. I wiped my brow in acknowledgment.

The entire shoot took under two hours, an amazing feat in the world of movies. I thanked him and began to head out, but I really didn't want to leave—I wanted to do more. I wanted just to hang around and be a part of the team. I managed to shuffle around for a few minutes. I realized that I was probably in the way and started to leave again. At the door, I glanced back at Tucci. Our eyes met, and I mouthed a final thank-you.

Alexis saw the little exchange and pulled me over closer to Stanley. "Would you like a Polaroid of the occasion?" Tucci was smiling from ear to ear—not that half-smile I had witnessed so many times earlier. He pulled me over, put his left hand on my shoulder, and said, "Take a few; I would like to have one, too." I was truly honored and moved by those words. Tucci is an actor, I am a freelance musician, and our worlds met on a quiet street in Brooklyn.

Joe Gould's Secret was released about a year later and ran on HBO for several months.

CHAPTER 18

Close Call

On your mark, get set ...

March 23, 1999: I am performing with the New Jersey State Ballet all week at the State Theater in New Brunswick. *Carmina Burana*, principal percussion duties, and the complete instrument rental for the production. Start making a list of all the instruments needed for these performances and see who will be performing in the section.

March 24: Took a call to play a series of concerts in Prague and surrounding countries next week. Even though this is short notice, I accepted. Check flight information, call airline, and confirm regular seat.

March 25: Called Czech Air, ticket confirmed; CSA from Newark. Flight departs Sunday, normal time, normal seat. I forgot how much equipment I need for the ballet concerts. Concerts are going well at the State Theater; performance time is two hours. Need to start packing for Sunday; bring new timpani mallets, passport, and overnight bag.

March 27: We have our final performance tomorrow at 2:00 p.m. in New Brunswick; the group sounds good.

What have I done? Tonight we lose one hour due to daylight savings time kicking in. *Call the airline!* Are we leaving at the normal time of 5:35 p.m., or 4:35 p.m.? If the flight leaves at 4:35, I don't see how I can possibly make it to the airport in time.

March 27, 10:00 a.m.: Worst fears confirmed: CSA flight is departing at

4:35. My concert will finish at 4:01 p.m. in New Brunswick! Thirty-four minutes to make it to Newark Airport is not possible.

Sunday, March 28: I am sitting on the plane as I type. The events, which have just concluded, are extraordinary to me.

After calling CSA and discovering the one-hour time change of my flight, I tried to find a replacement for my 2:00 p.m. performance in New Brunswick. But it was one of those Sundays where every percussionist on the east coast was working. I called all my friends and even my graduate students; no one was available.

From previous performances that week, I knew that the performance would last exactly two hours and one minute if we started on time. The trip from the theater to the Newark Airport is thirty minutes if there is zero traffic. This would get me to Newark International Airport by 4:31. Before the performance began, I spoke with the conductor and my section about my predicament. The conductor told me she would help out by beginning exactly at 2:00, not the respectful 2:05 for any latecomers. My good friend and percussionist Barry offered to pack up my rented instruments and drop them off at my studio. I accepted. He had a van and assured me my instruments were in good hands.

Due to the more-than-normal size of the production (including a large number of dancers and instrumentalists), additional stagehands were required to ensure the success of this production. As fate would have it, I knew one of them well. After explaining my situation to Denis, he reassured me that he would hold a parking spot for me at the stage door. With my car pointed north for a quick getaway, I felt more secure in my unbelievable challenge. The conductor instructed me not to wait for a bow or curtain call of any kind—"Just split" were her words. Before the final note had the chance to decay, I was out the door, in my car, and on my way.

My brother had come to the performance and had the car all set to go. Also, he would drive and drop me off at the airport, so I wouldn't have to put the car in long-term parking. Once I reached the car, my testosterone kicked in, and I told him to move over and let me drive. My brother drove fast, but I drove faster. He agreed and moved out of the driver's seat.

The contractor for this ballet lived down in South Jersey. She advised me not to take exit 14 (the one I was certain to take) to the airport, because I was coming up from the south. "Take 13A," she suggested. "It is more direct and should cut off a few minutes of travel time." I never took exit 13A but then again, I never travelled in from the south; it was always the north. I was hesitant to take her advice but reluctantly decided to place my trust in her suggestion.

I pushed the speedometer to a new high. I asked my brother to call ahead to the airport and ask for my favorite airline representative, Irka Jehlicka (Jehlicka means "needle" in Czech, and for good reason). When Miss Jehlicka picked up and heard of my emergency, she assured me the flight would be held. I had my brother ask Irka to have one of those motorized carts ready at the ticket counter to hustle me over to the departure gate. (In retrospect, it never would have happened this way in the wake of 9/11.)

After veering off the turnpike at Exit 13A, I pulled directly into the airport, cutting off several people in the process. Finally I arrived at the entrance for international departures. I hugged my brother and grabbed my bag. I darted inside, spotted the waiting cart, and jumped on; off we sped. As we hurtled down the corridor, Miss Jehlicka checked my passport and handed me a ticket for my usual seat, 2A. The entire time, the cart driver was on his walkie-talkie shouting, "Hold the door, hold the door!" Reaching the gate in record time, I jumped off, thanked my deliverers, and sprinted down the ramp. At the last few steps, I slowed down, trying to gain some composure. My hustle had been admirable, yet the entire business class section shot me a collective look that could kill. The gentleman sitting in 2B had all his personal belongings on my seat. Through the slits that resembled his eyes, his look said, "You have got to be kidding me." I asked him to remove his belongings so I could take my place.

The ever-attentive stewardess brought me a cold drink in one hand and a moist, warm, rolled-up mini towel in the other. After a moment or so, I felt refreshed. I opened the wonderful little package that CSA business class offered, filled with toothpaste, toothbrush, ear plugs, eye mask, cologne, deodorant, and my absolute favorite item, slippers. I removed the shoes covering my swollen feet and slipped on the little pieces of heaven.

By this time, I was completely in decompression mode. I knew we were moments, if not seconds, from taxiing to take off. It was then that it dawned on me: I remembered one of the percussionists had bet me twenty bucks that I wouldn't make it to the plane on time. Easy money.

Ironically, the plane, my business class companions, the couple of hundred in coach, and I have been sitting here now for nearly two hours. The door is jammed, and they cannot get it to fasten securely. It is now 6:20 pm, nearly two hours after the scheduled departure time.

CHAPTER 19

Precipice

It was the fall of 1998 when the music director of the Westchester Symphony called to make his request. I had been the personnel manager, as well as acting principal percussionist, of his orchestra. He called to let me know that the world premier we were about to perform that weekend required an additional percussionist. I thought to myself, *No problem, I can find someone to come in.* Before the thought could solidify in my mind, he requested that I call an old friend and colleague of his: David Fein. David was the principal percussionist of the New Jersey Symphony Orchestra, an orchestra I had wanted to play with for many years, but I never got the call. I couldn't imagine David would want to come and play with our orchestra, or even had the time to do so. Regardless, I tried to explain to Anthony what David's position was with the NJSO, and that I was principal of the Westchester Symphony Orchestra. Why would David want to come and play in the section, *my* section? I further explained how uncomfortable it would be for me, as the principal, to have to direct David if the occasion arose. Anthony listened attentively, but he definitely told me to call David for the gig before he hung up the phone.

What was I to do? I picked up the phone and called David to offer him the weekend of work. He accepted immediately. I told him what selections were on the program, as well as where we were rehearsing (Riverside Church in New York City). I did my best to welcome him to our orchestra.

The program included Prokofiev's *Romeo and Juliet Suite* as well as *Romeo and Juliet* by Tchaikovsky. As long as we had secured an additional player,

I invited David to play all works on the program that involved percussion. For the Prokofiev, I played the snare drum in all movements. Because the snare drum part is really exposed and requires a delicate touch, I chose an instrument from my vintage collection that allowed my sound to sing. The dynamic range of the work went from almost inaudible, ornamented strokes to extremely loud, smooth rolls, something which needed to be sustained over the entire orchestra.

For the Tchaikovsky, I played the solo cymbal part. My choice was eighteen-inch French hand-hammered Sabian cymbals: they were light in weight yet offered a crisp clash for each of the simulated sword strokes. David played the bass drum on the Tchaikovsky, offering an incredibly supportive approach to ensemble playing and displaying all the skills of a true team player.

During the weekend series, David and I chatted a good deal, getting to know each other through our conversation and musical interpretation. We discovered, among other things, that we shared the same taste in music and the same approach to performing. Generally speaking, we got along well, and our performance on Saturday night only added to the congenial atmosphere.

The following day, Sunday, I woke up, made a pot of coffee, and picked up the paper to see what was happening in the world. Just after my first sip, the telephone rang. As I picked up the phone and greeted the caller, my heart began to pump. On the other end of the phone was the personnel manager of the New Jersey Symphony Orchestra. He called to ask me if I was available to come and perform with the symphony beginning on Tuesday—this coming Tuesday. Of course I accepted, and I thanked him for the phone call. I remember thinking, *I guess I passed the audition this past weekend!*

My next thought took me back to my phone conversation with the music director. I recalled how I tried not to hire David for the concert, and how my entire life could have changed as a result of that phone call. The music director called me, I called David, and years later, I was the personnel manager of the New Jersey Symphony Orchestra. Unimaginable!

During my first few days with the New Jersey Symphony Orchestra, I performed on the snare drum, bass drum, cymbals, xylophone, field drum, glockenspiel, and tambourine. I was beginning to find my footing, and in the process I was actually enjoying myself! I remembered hearing that the NJSO was going through some difficulties in keeping percussionists on the roster. To date I am not sure why, but I would imagine that it had a lot to do with then Music Director Zdeněk Mácal.

My first few weeks with the NJSO were conducted by guest conductors, and everything seemed to be falling into place. Somewhere in my third week, I was asked to play an upcoming series that included *Copland Symphony No. 3*. Naturally, I accepted. I wanted to double-check the dates without bothering the personnel manager, so I walked to the musicians' bulletin board and looked up the series. There it was, in black and white: the dates, the times, and the fact that the series was being conducted by Mácal himself!

I prepared for the series very carefully, knowing where all my notes would fit in with the remainder of the orchestra; where to play my glockenspiel notes, my field drum notes, and rim shots—all in line with the rest of the section and orchestra. I felt really prepared. There was nothing left to do but wait for the first rehearsal, show up, play, keep my fingers crossed, and hopefully pass the Mácal test. If I passed, I could be engaged for future work.

The hour was at hand. Tuesday 10:00 a.m. came, and sure enough, at the appointed time Zdeněk walked onto the stage and moved directly to his podium. Without a word, he began conducting. My first entrance under his baton was to be played on the triangle. Believe me, I was nervous. I picked up my newly-purchased brass beaters (brass has less of an attack on the steel of the instrument) and produced my first note ever to hit his ear. At that moment, Zdeněk stopped the entire orchestra. I couldn't believe my eyes; what was he about to say? One note, and I was finished? It felt like my entire life flashed before my eyes. Never in a million years did I expect what came from his lips. He turned to David, the principal, and said "David, this is the sound I have been looking for; this is the sound, this, this!" Needless to say, I passed the Mácal test, and with flying colors. David was beaming from ear to ear.

Since that day some fourteen years ago, I have played nearly every triangle part in every piece we have performed, and I am extremely proud of it. I have built nearly my entire NJSO career as the solo triangle player. That is not to say that I have not covered every other percussion instrument needed along the way, but mostly my job has been to color the orchestral landscape using this bent piece of metal.

CHAPTER 20

Murphy's Law

Journal Entry: April 22, 2002

I found myself sitting at the bar of the Hotel Cueva del Fraile in Cuenca, Spain, reminiscing about years gone by. Cueva del Fraile is my favorite hotel in all of Spain. It is a former monastery that dates back to the sixteenth century, and it sits on six acres of land about seven kilometers into the mountains from downtown Cuenca. Cutting through the mountainside is the roadway that takes me back to past times, past feelings, past life. Although the hotel is tucked away in the middle of nowhere, it is just half a mile from the Arroyo de Bonilla River and a fifteen-minute drive from the famous Casas Colgadas hanging houses. The smell of the fresh, crisp air tickles the nose and is remarkably refreshing. No hustle and bustle of a busy life back home, no hectic work, no rapid movements. The only things one will find here are lots of peaceful surroundings, and the sound of birds waking up in the early hours to help greet the new day. The stillness of life up here is a far cry from the plans of my day, which include a concert at 8:30 p.m. in Valencia.

At the appointed time, I jumped into my rental car and onto the N-320, heading west toward Valencia. It was about a two and a half hour ride, which gave me plenty of time to think about the details and issues that might arise later that day. The trip was uneventful, less the brain exercises. I arrived at the church where the concert was to take place about four hours in advance of the scheduled sound check.

As I parked the car and approached the door, it became obvious that the church was small—*very* small. I was about to learn that the seating capacity was only 230 people. When I entered the church, although it was beautiful in appearance, it felt even smaller than I had imagined. The sanctuary, which we were to use as a makeshift stage area, was so small that we were barely able to put enough chairs across to fit the ensemble. I strategically began to place chairs and small benches into place, maneuvering them around structural pillars on the left and right of the sanctuary. Although some really unorthodox seating was arranged, in the final analysis I felt it was going to work. I kept an area clear for the percussion instruments, timpani, and drum set. As I was finishing with the complete setup, I realized that we were missing the piano, and I would need to make the proper room.

When traveling to Europe, it is usually easier to rent the larger instruments onsite, rather than ship them overseas. Prior to our trip, all arrangements were made with all the venues. Part of the agreement was for the venue to supply a piano. Looking back at the sanctuary, I was beginning to sweat as to where I was going to put it. I approached the pastor, who greeted me when I entered the church. "Padre, ¿dónde está el piano?" The good padre smiled and motioned for me to follow him. We started by walking from the sanctuary where the orchestra was to perform and headed, under the Gothic-style arches, past the left pillar, through the sacristy, down a hall, and finally up a narrow flight of stairs. I didn't like the thoughts that were going through my mind. We were heading up to the choir loft. I was thinking to myself as we were climbing the steps only one thought: *We can do this! We can have the pianist perform from the choir loft, just as they would if it were for a Sunday mass. The church is really small, and it could possibly work. It could be worse, no? It can work, it will work. It* must *work!*

In the loft, I looked around and saw three instruments, each one smaller than the next. In the center of the tiny loft sat a rather large organ that, judging from the inch of dust on it, wasn't functioning. The second instrument was a smaller version of the large organ, which was also not functioning. Then the prize. With a smile on his face, the priest uncovered a small, fifty-five-key keyboard. It was as if he was showing me the Holy Grail. I asked him if I could test out the instrument, and he nodded with approval. I turned the keyboard switch on and started to fiddle around with all the buttons, presets, and options that were available to me. At that moment, all I really wanted was to hear the sound of an actual piano, but no luck. Lots of organ, string, and woodwind sounds, but nothing that remotely mimicked a piano.

I felt really dejected and depressed, and I didn't know what I was going to do when the conductor and pianist arrived. I shifted my thoughts for the moment to how many tickets were sold. Before asking the padre, I looked around the church to see if I could spot any flyers announcing the evening performance. I didn't recall seeing any when I entered the church, which was normal in this concert venue setting. When I asked where all the publicity was, he informed me that there was no publicity. He continued to explain that this was not a benefit concert to help raise funds for the Valencia Red Cross (how it should have been advertised) or any other organization. I began to pull paperwork from my back pocket, stating the contrary, when I realized that my argument was not with the good padre but with my Spanish organizers. That fight would have to wait for another day. Padre further explained that he expected about twenty-five people; perhaps a few more would show up. What was I to do? The members of this orchestra had traveled thousands of miles to perform in Europe, and this was going to be their first experience. I had to think fast.

I needed to get to the Hotel Expo about fifteen minutes away on Avenida Pío XII, to meet the orchestra. We had arranged for them to stay close to the concert site, while I stayed in my sanctuary in Cuenca a few hours away. During my short ride from the church to the hotel, I came up with a plan. Admittedly it was a horrible plan—a really horrible plan—but what was I to do?

When I arrived at the hotel, I was greeted by our Spanish tour guides, Maria and Paloma. I asked them to gather the orchestra, board the bus, and begin making their way to the church for the sound check and subsequent concert. After directing our guides, I turned my head slightly to the right, only to see the face of the music director staring at me. Our eyes locked. It was obvious my face was telling a tale of uncertainty and dismay. It was time to put my horrible plan into motion, God forgive me! I began to explain how the associate pastor of this small church had a severe heart attack just a few days earlier, on Easter Sunday morning. The pastor wanted to cancel the concert out of respect for his ailing colleague. I also learned that during each of the morning masses, he had made the announcement that there was to be no concert in the evening. With that said, I suggested we proceed as planned, and use the evening's concert as a sort of live warm-up for the concerts yet to come.

I got back into my car and headed back to the concert venue, stressing over the lack of publicity, an organ for a piano, a broken bass, no extension cord, a smaller than small stage area, and more. I honestly felt like running back to my safe haven in Cuenca and forgetting about the entire affair.

When the orchestra arrived and set foot into the church, the youngsters all looked around in amazement; they were totally absorbed by the stunning Gothic art that surrounded them. They unpacked their instruments and began settling into their own performance space. I did not hear one complaint that there wasn't enough room. When the pianist took a look at the imitation keyboard she was to perform on, she looked at me and said, "Oh, this will do. I have one like this at home." With a few clicks, she transformed the keyboard into a not-so-bad-sounding piano. The conductor took up his baton, and the orchestra began running some of their selections.

What took place next was something just short of a miracle. When the people of this small suburb of Valencia heard the sound of music pouring out from the front doors and open windows of the church, people came out of their homes, off the street, and from the cafés, and they filled the church to capacity. By the start of the performance, we needed to add folding chairs in every conceivable location so that everyone could have a seat. There were Spaniards sitting in the choir loft among the dead, dust-filled organs. They were sitting behind the orchestra in the sanctuary, to their right and left, and under the pillars that towered over us. They were even in the percussion section as well!

The opening concert was a complete success, and one that I will remember for years to come.

CHAPTER 21

Chuck Berry

Journal Entry: December 7, 1999

Chuck Berry was coming to town to perform a one-night concert at the Morristown Community Theater (now the Mayo Center for the Performing Arts). The caller asked if I could provide the rhythm section for his performance. Once we agreed on the terms of the gig, it took less than twenty minutes to secure a bassist, pianist, and drummer.

On the day of the Berry gig, I was already scheduled to play a double rehearsal with a small chamber orchestra about twenty miles away. With this orchestra, we were going to perform the very popular *Messiah* by George Frederic Handel. The complete oratorio runs about three and a half hours if one played all movements of all three parts. For this particular performance, only the first part was chosen; about eighty minutes of music. Although we were only performing part one, it was customary to end with a selection from part two, the enjoyable and ever famous "Hallelujah Chorus." For me, the timpanist, there was a lot of sitting around until the finale, which lasted a total of five minutes. Admittedly, it was a glorious five minutes, with an equally glorious eighty-minute wait.

Regardless of the small assignment, I had been hired to attend a rehearsal at 1:00– 3:30 p.m. and again at 5:00–7:30 p.m. There was no way I could be in two places at the same time. I didn't want to give up *Messiah*, but I really wanted to attend a portion of the Berry rehearsal. I decided to take matters into my own hands. Before the rehearsal, I approached

129

the conductor and explained my situation. Because of this particular selection, its popularity, and having performed it at least a hundred times in the past, a miracle took place. All the pieces of the puzzle fit together, and for the first time in my career, a conductor accommodated a musician's need. He assured me I would not be needed for the evening rehearsal, and would still receive payment as originally agreed upon. *Wow, is this for real?* I soon learned he was good to his word. The personnel manager approached with the good news. We rehearsed, or shall I say, ran the "Hallelujah Chorus" near the end of the afternoon rehearsal; it was 2:45, and I was not needed for the rest of the rehearsal. Upon looking at my watch, I knew I would make it just after 3:00 to hear Chuck's rehearsal. Was it a miracle, fate, or something else? I don't know, but I got in my car and sped off to Morristown.

I arrived just after three to find the band in the green room, not on stage. I entered the green room and asked where Chuck was. They told me that he had gone back to his hotel. Perplexed I asked, "How did the rehearsal go?"

In unison they said, "It was only five minutes."

"Five minutes? What do you mean it was only five minutes?"

The drummer told me that Chuck had only one set of directions. "When I lift my right foot, you play, and when I put my foot down, you stop." He also added, "Everything is in the key of E, so don't get fancy on me." I was amazed at what I was hearing and had no choice but to digest and accept it. I took the musicians to the local watering hole and bought them lunch. Eight o'clock was still four and a half hours away.

Just before 8:00 p.m., the band took their places on stage. Once in place, they looked at each other with acknowledgment; they were ready. The drummer clicked his sticks together to set the tempo of the opening selection. The show had begun! They started a blues vamp in the key of E and waited for Chuck to make his entrance. They must have vamped for ten minutes before Chuck strode on stage. The tension was mounting, so when he finally graced us with his presence, the crowd went wild. The owner of the Morristown Community Theater and I were up in the lighting booth, watching. When he made his appearance, we popped open a nice bottle of Dom Perignon to help mark the occasion.

The concert was to last a minimum of one and a half hours. With about fifteen minutes remaining, I left the lighting booth, located in the back of the theater. I made a right out of the front doors and headed straight to the back of the theater. I gained access through the performers' entrance just off stage left. Once backstage, I was no more than ten feet away from this rock-and-roll icon. At that moment, I heard the all-familiar riff signaling the starting of "Johnny B. Goode." While listening and enjoying the sounds I grew up with, I noticed there was a woman standing in the wings, hovering around the area. As I crossed the backstage area, moving closer to her, she approached me with hostility. "Who are you, and why are you here?" My antennae up, I turned up the charm. I smiled and passed a comment about the greatness that was before my eyes, and then I told her that I had hired Chuck's backup band. It was only then that she smiled and moved a little closer.

Chuck played the tunes we all knew so well: "Maybellene," "Roll Over Beethoven," "Rock and Roll Music," and more. We sensed that he was beginning to wrap it up. We soon learned his final effort was to be a big jam—in E, of course. With no rehearsal, the band had to watch his right foot, right? It went up and they played; it went down, they stopped. As the jam went on and on, Chuck invited people from the audience to come up and join him on stage. This was a scary proposition, because dozens of fans, drunk or otherwise impaired, began to fill the stage. While people were dancing and the band played, somewhere in the middle of the tune, Chuck simply walked off stage. He unplugged his guitar and asked me to get the cord from his amplifier, still onstage. The band was still playing while he was already in his car and on his way down the road.

I hung around the post-concert reception, eagerly waiting to meet Chuck one on one. He never arrived. The band members and I took some photographs together, had a few drinks, told stories of the past few hours' events, and waited patiently to see if Chuck would reappear. An hour passed, so we all decided enough was enough and it was time to go home. As I arrived at my waiting car, parked just outside the backstage entrance, I noticed a red Cadillac pulling up. Inside was Chuck Berry, and he looked like he was more than ready to party. I didn't know where he had gone, I didn't know what he had been doing, but I did know who he was with. His female companion emerged from the passenger seat of the large vehicle. After hopping out of his car, he asked me where the party was. I put the keys back into my pocket and took them both upstairs to the reception area, where roughly fifteen people were still gathered. Photos were taken, and more champagne and cocktails were poured for all who remained. We stayed until the wee hours of the morning.

As the heat from the morning sunlight shone through my driver's side window, it slowly brought me back to reality. While rubbing the morning sand from my eyes, I realized I was in my van, still in the parking lot of the Morristown Community Theater.

CHAPTER 22

Fallen Apart

The bonds of love can never be diminished, ever

—The author

Journal Entry: February 12, 2004

I have been going through a very difficult period. I have had no time to do anything but focus on work. I realize everyone has his own level of tolerance, but in the past few months, I have been tested to the maximum. Adding to my personnel manager duties, I was performing each week anywhere from eight to ten services in the percussion section. The stress of wearing both hats nearly became unbearable. In addition to my workload, Arts Alive was going through a very nasty New Jersey State tax audit. These factors contributed to making me feel as if the walls were caving in all around me. I was not sleeping well, and in retrospect I was not taking very good care of myself. Like a perfect storm, all the pieces of this very delicate puzzle were aligning; I was on a collision course with fate.

On that particular morning, I woke up feeling as if there was a two-ton weight on my chest. My head was throbbing at a rate I had never experienced, and I was having difficulty catching my breath. Yes, I was scared. I attempted to prepare for the day ahead of me, but my nerves began to unravel even more. I felt unsteadiness all about me, generated from deep within my being. This was something I had never experienced before. I was too wobbly to stand, so I moved to the nearest seat. I began to take very slow, exaggerated, deep breaths, trying desperately to settle down. After repeating this exercise for several minutes, I began to feel my body and mind calm down. Several minutes later, I cautiously rose from the chair. Still unsteady, I thought about calling an ambulance to take me to the hospital for a checkup. Blaming all my problems on fatigue, I talked myself out of a checkup and instead got in my car and headed off to work.

At 8:15 a.m., I pulled out of my driveway to begin my fifteen-minute ride to the New Jersey Performing Arts Center (NJPAC) in Newark. Still feeling woozy, I placed a call to my brother John. Although it was early in the morning, and I wasn't sure if he was even awake, I dialed his number anyway. John was a year older than me, and I would often call him for so many reasons, but especially when I was experiencing internal difficulties. He answered my call and immediately began with his intuitive comments. As always, his instincts were right on, and I found him to be miraculous in his approach to help. He asked why I sounded so shaky, quickly reminding me that shaking was his job, assigned by Parkinson's (he always poked fun at his own condition). In a way only a brother could, he spoke words of advice and listened to me during what felt like a three-hour trip to work.

When I arrived at the guest entrance gate at the NJPAC, he heard me say, "Jim Neglia, New Jersey Symphony" to the little black transmitter that leads to the guards' office. I was admitted just like every other morning. John joked that if he were to go to the backstage gate, he too could be admitted, because we shared the same voice. By the time we finished our conversation, I was feeling much better and much more centered. Once parked in my waiting spot, he concluded his pep talk. I thanked him in some ridiculous, nonsensical way and shut the engine down.

I made my way into the building through the large double-glass doors, waved to the attending guard, and headed straight for the production office. The production office was located between the musicians' lounge and our concert stage, Prudential Hall. Once there, feeling somewhat refreshed, I placed my bags down on the empty table. When I turned around, I saw that one of the musicians had followed me into the room.

Tom and I hit it off and became good friends from the time I had first joined the NJSO as a substitute percussionist seven years earlier. Tom was about sixty-eight years young and was as sharp as one could imagine. He absolutely knew that something was wrong when he saw me walk into the building and to the office. When I swung around, Tom and I were standing face to face. After exchanging our normal morning salutations, I suddenly lost my balance and fell into the wall. Tom helped me into a chair and discretely closed the door of the production office. I broke down completely and began crying uncontrollably. I was shaking, my head was spinning, and I felt as if my legs would never be strong enough to get me out of my seat again. I was experiencing something I couldn't understand or accept, yet it was happening, and on a very large scale.

Tom stayed with me but said very little; he would parentally stroke my back every few seconds as my head leaned against his side. My current workload, coupled with the horrible audit, helped push me to the brink of no return, or at least greatly contributed to my current state. But the truth hurt even more: it wasn't until that particular moment that I felt my real pain, the actual realization, the anguish all around me. In an instant, I understood everything I was feeling. I was beginning to digest the truth. My brother, who was deteriorating from various ailments, was the one I always called when in real distress. It was John who always found a way to comfort me, refocus me on the road to recovery. It all came into focus precisely at that moment, crystal clear in my understanding. John would die from his dreaded diseases, this was certain. For the first time, I began to understand if not accept the inevitable. I have no idea why it took me so long to recognize. Once I heard myself say it out loud to Tom, I knew it was true, real, and undeniable. My brother, whom I loved and shared everything with, would die, sometime sooner rather than later. How was it possible? This happened to other families, not ours. It wasn't possible.

That day at work was perhaps the longest of my career.

––––––––––––––––––

Since then, I settled my audit. This alone took an enormous weight off my shoulders. Although I was found guilty of the charges levied against my little company, I worked out a very good settlement with the state.

The enormous pressure of the audit was over. With its departure came what appeared to be a more palatable work load. In reality, even though nothing actually lessened at the work place, everything seemed to lessen. What came to mind clearly and didn't change was my brother and his sickness. For the next several years, John would be part of my daily reality check. All the time I knew, understood, and even began learning how to accept what was to come.

His sickness helped me to realize how blessed my life had been over the years. I had learned compassion, understanding, and acceptance on so many levels. Through John's sickness I learned to reach out to those in need, wanting to help where able. How precious life was, and how important love could be. The bonds of a close family could bind us both in this life and the next.

On January 9, 2010, a multitude of ailments led to a massive heart attack that took John from us. The pain and collapse I experienced in February 2004 was nothing compared to the stabbing pain I experienced that day. I watched him pass before my eyes. I lost my brother, my band mate, confidant, best man, and friend. Although for some time I had expected the inescapable phone call, when it finally came that dreaded morning, I crumbled. It was the most difficult acceptance I had lived through to date. At 5:00 a.m. I rushed to the hospital, hoping beyond hope. But once I saw him, I knew in my heart he was gone. On life support, his body lay still for a few precious hours more until he began his new journey.

Since John's passing, I have offered so many performances to him, on occasions where I thought he really would have enjoyed a particular selection of music. Among his favorites were most, if not all, of the Beethoven symphonies, *Appalachian Spring*, and Brahms' *Symphony No. 4*. But perhaps at the top of his list was the famed Mozart *Requiem* (the Süssmayr version). During his decline, when he was unable to perform as an organist and singer, he took refuge in recreating classical selections digitally, on the computer. I have many memories of his digital offerings of dozens of classical works. But the one that he was very proud of was Mozart's *Requiem*. As each movement of the requiem was completed,

I would receive an e-mail with an MP3 attachment for my listening pleasure. What pride he took in the process and ultimately the final product.

If I had a penny for every time I reached for my phone to share with him some event, concert, Seinfeld comment, *Godfather* reference, or just what was happening in my life, I could have retired already. At times I would continue with my fictitious call, hoping he would feel my desire to continue to share with him. John was my older brother, and to this day I miss more than words can ever express.

Knowing John, I am sure he will never allow his memory to be diminished. Constant reminders of his likes and dislikes, both musically and otherwise, enter my thoughts daily. Apart from sharing my musical offerings with him, John reminds me to remain centered and focused each day of my life, the same way he did in 2004. I know he is with me; at times, I can hear his voice ringing in my ears, as well as his jabbing, poking, tongue-in-cheek comments. His memory remains with me most pronounced each morning when I arrive at work and press the little silver button on the intercom announcing my arrival. I can hear a soothing laugh in my ears. "I can get past the gate because we share the same voice."

My views and feelings are best summed up in the following passage from Edward Abbey's *Cold Mountain*.

> You could grieve endlessly total loss of time and for the damage done therein, for the dead, and for your own lost self. But what the wisdom of the ages says is that we do well not to grieve on and on. And those old ones knew a thing or two and had some truth to tell. For you can grieve your heart out and in the end you are still where you were. All your grief hasn't changed a thing. What you have lost will not be returned to you. It will always be lost. You're left with only your scars to mark the void. All you can choose to do is go on or not. But if you go on, it's knowing you carry your scars with you.

CHAPTER 23

Czech Love

Journal Entry: April 5, 2001

Truman Capote once wrote that he believed that anybody who loved somebody else and pursued them ardently enough would eventually "get" them, for no one can resist being loved!

I am home; great trip with no real problems. Highlights included performances with the Czech Radio Symphony. They were great fun and extremely fulfilling. The members of the orchestra took me in as one of their own without hesitation. I had been listening to Czech language study aids for several months, and I knew a few phrases as well as my numbers, days of the week, and how to say, *"Where is the bathroom?"* I made every effort to fit in, and it was obvious to them. They knew I came to be part of their family, not just to play a gig. Along with my attempt to communicate in Czech was my very American approach to music performance, which was also very well accepted by my European friends. The universal language helped bridge the gap between my bad Czech, their good English, and many wonderful performances.

After the tour, I decided to stay and take my holidays throughout Europe. Beginning where the tour ended, I began my lazy days in Budapest. Afterward I headed west for a few hours to Vienna and then to Linz. After a week in Austria, I headed north to the amazing village of Český Krumlov, located in southern Bohemia. After a few relaxing days there, I headed northeast to Moravia and the city of Brno, where I met up with some longtime friends. We enjoyed some great meals, conversation, and plenty of pivo! My final destination was northwest of Brno: my home base and beloved city, Prague.

I spent a good deal of time making my way around this corner of the globe, absorbing all it had to offer. I love traveling, exempt of any and all fears. I enjoyed meeting all the new faces, seeing the sights, and walking the streets of deep-seated history. I found myself mesmerized by my now-familiar surroundings. Staroměstské náměstí, better known as Old Town Square, was located between Wenceslas Square and the famous Charles Bridge, one of the most beautiful places I have ever visited. It was here that I would find myself alone most of the time, usually deep in thought. Eyes scanning the cobblestone blocks, long bridges, wonderful monuments, and the general hustle and bustle of this vibrant area—I was in my glory. It was during this particular stretch of downtime that I came to the realization that I needed to drastically change my life.

Journal Entry: April 3, 2001, 11:30 a.m.

I am at the *Ruzyně* airport in Prague, waiting to depart for the States. My dear friends Kaja and Pavla dropped me off. As we said our good-byes, the pain hit me hard as I realized how very sad I was to be leaving. Prague had quickly become a place where I envisioned myself living. I love it here and don't want to go back to the States—not now, and perhaps not ever. With each departure, time and time again the inevitable truth of leaving sank in. I was leaving a place that made me feel at ease, comfortable, peaceful, at home, and very welcome. I love being in Prague, and at this moment I wished I would never return to the States—a place where I had to work, defend my position, struggle, network, and push as hard as one could imagine.

Prague was not only a wonderful and welcome home, but it was also an amazing place to make music. Music was all around me; the great orchestras of Prague were asking me to come back to perform with them time after time. How could I refuse their requests, never mind my own desire to return? In Prague I felt uninhibited and always able to act, feel, and be as I felt I should feel in the moment. I played neither games of position nor the game of musical politics. I was just Jim, the timpanist who felt as if I were a real native of Europe, not America. I loved the feeling that showered me each time I set foot on European soil: it was a feeling of belonging, needing, wanting, acceptance, and comfort.

I loved my life overseas, and each return to the States only brought me anxiety, suffering, and longing for a place I wanted desperately to call my new home. I went as far as to solicit an apartment just off Old Town Square, a block and a half away: Kožná 110 00, a one-bedroom apartment that made my heart skip a beat. It was a place I could call my own. But as an American, the red tape to purchase was so thick that it hampered my push to adapt to Czech life in its fullest. All these experiences and feelings came flooding back each time I visited Prague. However, it was my departure that would tend to make me crumble like there was no tomorrow.

As I was walking through the airport, heading for the gate where familiar Flight 052 was set to take off, I was really feeling blue. I was attempting to sort through my feelings, falling short of the reality of leaving. Faintly, in the background, I could hear REM playing the familiar tune "Everybody Hurts." *How perfect, how profound*, I thought. I was barely able to deal with my own hurt, which the lyrics so perfectly spoke: "When your day is night alone, hold on. If you feel like letting go, hold on." Hang on was all I had to do, and of course I did.

Over the years, I have spent a great deal of time traveling, mostly alone; I was never bothered by the solitude. While alone, I was allowed to get lost in my thoughts and drift far away from my other life so many miles away. It was my desire to record these thoughts that led me to the nearest café, park, or hotel lobby to jot down my innermost feelings of the moment.

On the flight home I wrote,

> I miss Prague all the more this time around. I feel as if my life is really in crisis mode, unsure of the moment and future that lies before me. I have serious moments of doubt that I would make it back to New Jersey and stay for more than enough time to pack my bare essentials and make the journey back to the Golden Jewel. This feeling is overwhelming! This could change my life

in every possible way. What would my family think? Will I ever see them again? What do I really need to take with me? I could sell all my possessions—furniture, car, nearly everything—and begin anew. I am sure I can do it and will find success in Europe. I am feeling extremely lonely and isolated.

A few hours later:

Nothing would be the same for me. I am not even sure of what it is I am looking for, but if I find it, what makes me think that it will be any better or different from what I have now in the States? I have been so confused over the past eight months; I am not sure what is right and what is wrong. I am unhappy and uncertain, not sure how I want to change, yet I feel change is inevitable. My heart is always open and vulnerable, but this time I am truly in pain at the thought of leaving my beloved Prague. I remind myself that separation is a desperate action for me these days. Why do I continually put myself through this painful process, this agony month after month? [I was referring to my multiple, constant trips abroad, week after week, month after month, and by now, year after year.]

A few weeks passed when I received a letter from a valued friend, one in whom I had confided about the uncertainty of my life. Her response:

Can you imagine all the other times you have metamorphosed over the years and maybe not noticed? Or forgotten about it entirely? The old Jim is definitely a composite being—and actually the new person you are discovering in yourself will eventually become assimilated after you someday realize so much of the old still exists, too. Sometimes you just get really defining events in your life that necessitate redefining yourself to keep living; you have a lot of those happening right now. I think you really just have to go with the change, and not try to make the old stuff work for you anymore. Keep what's good, and clear the rest out.

A few months later I recorded some updated thoughts.

Journal Entry: August 18, 2001

The road to recovery can sometimes be a long and undefined one. Who knows what life has in store for us? Over the past few months, I have learned how to live a fearless life. Once all fears have been abandoned, that is when we can start to live fully, with no expectations, needs, wants, or desires that will complicate our lives—just a pure love of life and clearer vision into one's self.

I remember the torture I lived through back in 2001. My feelings were real and, at the time, very much present. All these years later I can see why I was lost and what was at the very root of my unhappiness. I was desperate to change my life and ultimate direction. Most of those feelings were shadowed by uncertainty and confusion. At the time, escape from my current life consumed my thoughts. I was searching for a new life. In Europe, I felt wonderful, never alone, and always embraced by work and people who surrounded me. I will never know how it would have turned out if I had followed my dream and moved to Prague, but I have no regrets in staying put.

In the years that followed those journal entries, I see where my life was and where I have arrived all these years later. Once my fears were abandoned, life truly began anew. It took nearly four decades to understand my absolute place in life. Ultimately I heard the message loud and clear. The message I learned had nothing to do with my geographic location, but my inner mind-set and peace. After years of searching for life's mysteries, I learned not to look any further than my own soul.

CHAPTER 24

Friendship

July 9, 2003

Greetings to You, Ray,

Thank you ever so much for the beautiful card you and Margie sent to me. I feel the same way about the two of you. Do you remember the writing on the card you sent?

> I believe that God brings certain people into our lives for a reason. Sometimes it's to help us see something new and wonderful, sometimes it's to encourage us and strengthen our purpose, and sometimes it's just to remind us that we are never truly alone and that it is important to share our smiles, our dreams, and even our tears …

> (On the inside): Whatever reason He had in bringing us together, I'm very glad that He did. You have been a real source of understanding and happiness in my life and you matter very much to me—more than any words could really say.

I hope the rather long letter I sent a few weeks ago met your satisfaction. I really enjoy writing these days, and documenting my life as it unfolds. [Referring to my trip to Kerrville,] I reread the letter I sent to you and realized I could have written even more! I feel I left so much out. There was one point I omitted that I did add in after I sent you that long account of my trip: while we were at lunch, and you took my left hand while Margie took my right. You offered up the most beautiful prayer imaginable, one of love, grace, and friendship. There we sat in a busy restaurant, among what appeared to be hundreds of people, yet we were indeed alone in our little circle of friendship and prayer. I tell you, Ray, this was a beautiful moment that I will cherish forever. Thank you again for allowing me into your lives and embracing our friendship as no other has.

CHAPTER 25

Chuck

We all have people in our lives who have contributed to our growth and development; it is rare when that person remains with you for more than a select period of time. Below, you will see how a single person defied the passage of time and continues to impact my life, even to this day.

There was another person who was an enormous influence in my life. It was a person whom I grew to love almost immediately from the first time we met. There are very few relationships, apart from family, that have sustained the test of time. They're not so common, in my opinion. The question is, how do these relationships actually begin? Are both people cognitively aware of some unmistakable void? How much energy and desire is needed to sustain the relationship? What is the ultimate objective? I can tell you that regarding this relationship, I am able to answer all these questions with absolute certainty.

I have been blessed to have had such a relationship in my life with someone other than a family member. I have a person who really gives a darn about my well-being, family, working conditions, life in music, and so much more. Having unconditional love from my family is not even a consideration in my mind. But when a stranger decides to take you under their wing, you have to stop and reflect on their motivation.

In the fall of 1984, I began my studies at the Mannes College of Music in New York City. The building was located on Seventy-fourth and Lexington Avenue, in the heart of the east side of Manhattan. I loved it there; I absolutely belonged to the inner fabric of the school. I had been accepted into the Manhattan School of Music, as well as the Juilliard School, but it was Mannes who offered me a partial scholarship and work-studies program. I accepted their generous offer and began my studies. I was paying for my own education and felt this was where I needed to be, and also where I could afford to study.

As with Ray in Texas, to this very day I have remained in touch with the president of the Mannes College of Music, from when I began my studies so many years ago. I have come to rely on his advice, listen to his input, and act on his years of knowledge and experience. I have asked him for assistance on several life-altering issues; from the Arts Alive audit, NJSO issues, and job offers from around the globe. I shared all this while keeping him abreast of my personal life.

There are times when I would receive an e-mail from him that simply read, "So?" When I would receive such an e-mail, I knew it was time to respond immediately. I remember in 2005, I entered my NJSO office to find the red light blinking in the lower left-hand portion of my phone. When I checked my answering machine, I heard his voice stating, "You have twenty-four hours to contact me, or else!" This was a serious message that warranted an immediate response—no screwing around, nothing more pressing. I would drop everything and pick up the darn phone.

Each morning of my Mannes tenure, I would arrive at the school no later than 7:00 a.m. Finding a parking spot was relatively easy, because I had come to know exactly who drove to work and who didn't. I would camp out next to the car I knew would pull out with the least amount of waiting time. Once parked, I would go to the corner restaurant and grab a bagel and a cup of coffee. Less than two minutes later, I would hit the buzzer on the outside of the building to gain entry. At that hour, there were no signs of life in sight, with the exception of one: the president of the college.

Once through the door, I would need to pass his office in order to make my way to the right and down the hall to the percussion room. In the beginning, the mornings were uneventful: walk in, pleasant greetings, and down to the business of warming up and preparing for the day's rehearsals and lessons. It wasn't until a few weeks had passed when Chuck saw my obvious commitment to my art and studies. By the beginning of October, when he would let me in, he began to make little jokes with me, like, "Did your mother throw you out again?" or some other tongue-in-cheek remark that forced me to stop in my tracks and laugh.

One morning when I entered the building, he noticed that I was in a bit of a hurry, because I barely said good morning. "Hey, what's up? Are you okay?" I explained that I wanted to hear a selection of music that was to come on the radio at 7:03 a.m. At the time, WQXR published their playing program monthly, and I was a very happy subscriber. It was his turn to laugh, but he offered to let me listen in his office, which was closer than the percussion room. As I entered his office, the radio was already tuned to WQXR, and the work began nearly immediately. I took a deep breath and sank into a rather large leather chair. I popped open my coffee and sipped slowly, savoring every sip as well as every note played. It wasn't until I had been there for several minutes that I came out of my cocoon and looked up. Chuck was sitting at his desk, working diligently on the *New York Times* crossword puzzle, sipping his coffee as well. This process repeated itself daily for the next four years.

Each morning was identical to the day before, with one exception: our conversation. I quickly came to look forward to our few morning minutes together. On so many occasions we spoke of music, what I was working on that particular week, and what was coming up next. Other conversations were based on my family and upbringing. He took an honest, caring approach to our conversations. I learned about his wife and three boys, the things he enjoyed doing, and his philosophies on so many issues, including how to obtain one's true goals. Our conversations never lasted more than ten minutes—after all, I had practicing to accomplish. As he finished his puzzle, I would begin to wind down the morning thoughts and take my leave.

I learned so much while exposed to his genuineness and obvious, thoughtful manner. Many of his teachings of compassion filtered through to my current thought process. I draw on the conversations of all those years ago when dealing with my everyday work, as well as my personal life. Even after my college days were over, we remained in touch, but of course on a much more limited level. However, in times of extreme crisis or joy, I would find myself jotting him an e-mail to share the current event. We shared these events, as well as work situations, and the loss of friends and colleagues (which I found extremely difficult). Job offers and job securities were up for discussion as well. After all, it was Chuck who talked me through the interview process for my current position. We shared a great deal of history together, and I felt his responses are worthy of sharing with you in the excerpts below.

On being offered the personnel manager position:

October 31, 2003
The job is mine.

Wheeeee! Congratulations! I am really happy for you, and I am happy that the orchestra showed such excellent judgment. Good for them, too. But don't expect any more respect, because now you are a big-shot manager!

Chuck, thank you for all your support through this process. I couldn't possibly think of a better person to share my misery with than you, you lucky guy. In all sincerity, I want you to know how much I appreciate your friendship, advice, and concern for me and my career. You are and always will be a special person in my life, and I will continue to cherish our long-lived partnership.

I am here all the time, and I don't know anyone, except maybe my grandsons, that I would rather talk with. Bravo! Whatever you did must have been right!

November 3, 2003
And remember what I said in my last message, unpleasant as it sounds: Alertness + eyes and ears in the back of your head + keen observation = the doorway to survival and success!

May 20, 2003
I can't tell you how moved I was by your letter, and how grateful I am to you for the thoughts that you expressed. When your career is over, it's good to hear that you were of some consequence to someone along the line. I also can't tell you how impressed I am with what you have built during the last twenty years—who can believe that it has been that long? Wasn't it all last week? I can remember it all with complete clarity.

November 23, 2003
I realize my next statement may seem a bit odd, but just hear me out! During my performances this week, I have taken on a new sense of

security, absolute confidence. Is it just because I have a job? I am playing better than ever; no fears or anxiety, no nerves, no nothing. Christ, it feels good! I am also aware that this is the honeymoon, and the marriage is just beginning. However, this short period of time has renewed my inner peace on so many levels.

Feels good, huh? Wouldn't it be a gas to read through all your e-mails during the interview/search process?

November 27, 2003
There was *no* reason to remind me of all our e-mail exchanges prior to getting the gig. I assure you!

It was not a reminder; it was a comment about the environment in which you lived during that time.

I don't think I could (will) ever forget the anxiety and discomfort I went through.

Old expression: "nothing comes for nothing!"

I have kept every e-mail that has gone back and forth via the information highway in my trusty journal. It will make a great book one day—well, at least for my own enjoyment.

The most difficult aspect of accepting the job has been canceling all other outside playing obligations. A day or so after accepting the job, it became obvious that I needed to clear my prior performance schedule. On that fateful afternoon, I spent three or four hours on the phone, offering my percussion friends all of my work through August 2004. I handled the phone calling like a well-oiled machine, methodically offering each job away, gig by gig. It wasn't until after all substitutes were secured that I realized I had just passed along fifteen years of hard-earned, well-managed freelancing gigs. Fifteen years of building up a work base from which I lived. Yes, I was sad, but I knew I had done the right thing.

Yes, and you knew that this was an inevitability if you got the job. Well, all's well that ends well—right? I have to tell you that it really is good to hear you sounding the way that you sound. You have always been a hard worker and a dedicated professional, but unfortunately in this society, that doesn't always pay the rent. It's comforting and rewarding and reassuring to see that it has for you. Bravo! Onward and upward!

I have truly been blessed in so many ways. (I am in thanksgiving mode.) I am thankful for the grounding I learned at Mannes through you and others who made a major impact on my life. Rest assured, you are at the top of my list. I am thankful that I have learned to not be afraid, to not give up, and to bust my ass always. The rewards will come to me tenfold.

Exactly right. In the last analysis, despite what you went through and with whom you went through it, it is you who steered the ship and decided what had to be done, and then did it.

What a great feeling it is to wake up in the morning and feel so good. The pressure and stress of life is at a minimum, even with the new job. I am grateful that my Arts Alive clients aren't abandoning ship. Pinch me, I am still in disbelief.

Be grateful! This is what is called a good plan, well-executed, and no one fired any torpedoes at it. Good for you! Onward and upward! You are a good guy!

December 4, 2003
Well, well, well birthday boy!

Yeah, right! Some "boy"!

I am extending my most sincere (belated) wishes to you on your birthday. Seventy-five …

Thank you, thank you, still a long way to go.

The way I see it, I will need my mentor for many years to come, and who better to call upon than you.

I am here—so far!

Who else has a no-holds-barred ability to keep me in line!

Nah … You're always in line. You're too smart to get too far out of line. It helps everybody to have someone to talk to.

I know I have said this about a million times in the past few months, but I would like to restate the obvious. I am so very happy we rekindled our once-shared friendship. Your words carry the same weight as they did so many years ago. How refreshing to hear honest (if not painful at times) remarks and advice from you. I can never get tired of your continued generosity and willingness to hear my story.

I repeat—I am here, and I enjoy back-and-forthing with you. Well, I'll tell you—I am impressed but not at all surprised. Just great! I could not be happier for you. How about taking a look at the e-mails that we exchanged during the weeks that the interview process, etc. was being sweated out? I bet that there are some life lessons in there. Happiness!

January 24, 2004
Well, that was a big dose. But it all sounds pretty routine for a responsible officer of administration in a major arts venue—they ain't paying you for your good looks. And it also sounds as though it is very interesting and very challenging and equally rewarding. And it also sounds as though you have it by the neck and are doing just fine, which does not surprise me at all.

Remember, change is constant and usually beneficial. We all have to develop! Get yourself overtired, and judgment suffers!

Jim, I really am happy for you. I remember very well how uptight, tense, nervous, and a little unsure you were in the weeks before you got the job. You are a good guy, and you deserve what you have achieved. Bravo.

August 7, 2007
So there it is: a short wrap-up of the past few months. Although I am sharing with you a mere fraction, all is documented in my personal journal. One day, the book will write itself.

No, it won't.

CHAPTER 26

A Missing Bass Cable

Journal Excerpt: April 19, 2003, Barcelona, Spain

During one of my musical tours to Europe, I was faced with a unique problem that required swift resolution. To resolve a problem in theory can be easy, but the practical side took some doing. I needed to consider all the possibilities. Once I figure out a strategic plan for settling these unforeseen circumstances, I put the wheels in motion. On this trip, I had one of those issues that no matter what I did, I could not fully resolve the issue. I felt as if I had lost the battle, and I hate to lose.

On this particular tour, I was faced with the task of setting up concerts for four separate groups who were all traveling together. These four groups performed their own varied repertoire, but they wanted to perform a few selections together as one large, combined force. It sounded good to me, but finding suitable venues for such a diverse group took some real ingenuity and a lot of persistence with my counterparts in Europe. Once the concert venues were secured, I began to focus more on pre-departure efforts.

A jazz vocal group, a concert choir, a string orchestra, and a jazz big band—a total of eighty-seven total performers—were all slated to depart for a concert tour of Spain. As the organizer of such a large event, I needed to have all the key ingredients in place. This included arranging airline tickets, hotels, meals, concert venues, luggage requirements, sightseeing, bilingual guides, buses, instrument-hauling trucks, and more. Although I do all the major organization for these trips, it falls upon the duties of the performing group to have their act together as well. They need to provide me with names of participants, passport numbers, instrument requirements, rooming lists, dietary requirements, and so much more. Fortunately, this group had traveled with Arts Alive in the past, and we enjoyed a good working relationship. I set up a pre-departure schedule of all our needs, which was provided to my clients.

I am not so foolish to think for a fleeting moment that any performance tour will go off without a hitch. It is a given that something will go wrong—it is an absolute certainty. However, with years of touring experience under my belt, I feel that I am able to head off most of the unforeseen. With that said, the particular problem of this tour unfolded soon after our touchdown in Barcelona. The problem was not as easily resolved as I would have liked.

The airline I chose for this trip was TAP, Air Portugal. I was able to secure cargo space for five celli, two contrabasses, and all the percussion equipment at no additional cost to me or my clients. I have some very effective methods of working with airlines that will ensure complete satisfaction on my part. The five cello cases and the two coffin-like bass cases are very large, and they require proper handling at all times. In addition to the special handling, proper flight cases are essential. In New York, we have been fortunate to deal with an organization that provides such cases and helps ensure a secure method of travel for the instrument inside.

In addition to the large string instrument and percussion cases, I was in search of a good price on other rental items. We needed to supply bass and guitar amplifiers. After researching these two items for possible rental while in Spain, I discovered that it would be more cost-effective to rent them here in the States and ship them with the other large items. Once again, I called Air Portugal and made the necessary arrangements. I searched out a local rehearsal studio in Manhattan, where I secured the amplifiers and flight cases. At an agreed-upon time, the rental outfit dropped off the items at Newark International Airport for the awaiting flight.

At the airport, the amplifiers passed through customs without incident. The bass and cello cases needed to be unlocked and remain that way through the load-in process. The events of September 11 were still felt years later. Once it was discovered that there was nothing stowed in the large cases, they were secured. The airline officials fastened the loosened locks and passed the cases through to cargo. The next time we saw the cases was at El Prat airport in Barcelona the following morning. As we collected our luggage and cases, we passed through the next stage of our trip: customs on the European side. All the paperwork was in order, and we breezed through.

It was a long and extremely turbulent flight, and by the time we landed, we were all exhausted from our travels. As we boarded the bus, I saw the instrument-moving truck was also being loaded. Within a few minutes, we were headed for our hotel forty minutes away. It wasn't until the following day, April 18, that the real nightmare would begin.

The group's first performance was scheduled for April 19, one day away. The director of the jazz ensemble asked me if I could secure a room where the ensemble could warm up. No problem, as I had already made these arrangements prior to our departure. The musicians were eager to play their instruments and to begin rehearsing for their rather large scheduled event for the following day.

I watched the kids set up the drum kit and unpack the guitar and bass amplifiers. When the bassist took the protective lid off the amplifier, he discovered that there was no power cord supplied. I got up and told him to look under the power switch, which was tucked underneath the half-open back. No luck; the cord was not there. It was about 8:30 a.m. in Spain, making it 2:30 p.m. New York time. I pulled out my cell phone and dialed overseas to the rehearsal studio that provided the amplifier. After a series of questions, it was admitted by my suppliers that the cord had been left behind in New York.

I stressed the importance of this cable, because our concert was set for the following evening at 9:00 p.m. I told them to call DHL or some other guaranteed delivery service and get me that cable. But the rehearsal studio had a better idea, which I later found out. RS Studio chose to send the cable on a commercial flight with Iberia airlines. Why? To this day I still don't understand. Iberia charged seventy-five dollars to fly the cable over, whereas DHL or FedEx would have been comparable. LP Studio faxed all the paperwork to me that should make my pick-up in Spain painless. They were wrong. It was Friday, and not just any Friday but Good Friday, and I need my cable now! Patience … tomorrow I would go back to the airport, meet the incoming Iberia flight, grab the cable, and be back before the rehearsal starts.

On Saturday, I hailed a cab and made my way to El Prat airport, about forty minutes from the center of the city. When we pulled up to the international arriving flights drop-off area, the cabby stopped the car. I paid the sixty Euros, took a receipt, and let the driver go on to his next fare.

I walked up to the Iberia help counter only to find there was no help waiting for me. I was doing my best to explain the situation, but our language barrier prevented the complete story from coming out. I realized that I needed to hand over the paperwork to help complete my story. She looked at me with confusion in her eyes, like I should have known where to go. "No non qi, or heeere. You go cargo." She passed the paperwork back to me, and I left the counter and began looking for the cargo area. I walked around the airport for a few minutes reading signs, but with no luck. Then I saw a customs official milling about. He was able to help me and told me that the cargo area was about seven kilometers outside the airport. In a huff, I went back to the taxi area and hailed another cab, which took me to the proper location.

Once we arrived at the cargo area, a whole new set of circumstances arose. Looking around as we pulled up, I begged the driver to wait for me. "Por favor, no me dejes!" I refused to pay him, to help ensure that he would stay while I went about my business.

When I walked into the cargo building, I noticed at least six workers behind the counter. All of them were sipping their coffee and ignoring everything else around them—including me. I respectfully waited a few minutes before I put a halt to their break. In doing so, I was greeted with hostility. Not until I produced the invoice for the cable was I helped. It was then that a worker walked up to me. He asked if I was an American, and I nodded in acknowledgment. He told me, "I speak a little English. Please, how may I help you?" I was so happy to get some real service that I was able to explain the day's events in just five or six sentences. I was careful to leave out anything that had to do with the lack of help I had received thus far.

He looked into my eyes with understanding and sympathy. "*Signore,* I am sorry, but the flight will not be in from Madrid for another two hours." By now it was nearly 3:30 p.m., and I simply didn't have another two hours to kill. Our concert was five and a half hours away, back in the center of Barcelona. I was faced with no choice, so I decided it would be best if I waited. I told the kind Spaniard that I would wait until 5:00 or 5:30 for the cable. He retorted, "Oh, I am sorry, we close at 4:00 p.m. But we will be back at 7:00 a.m. Tuesday morning."

What? By Tuesday we would be in the province of Valencia, 365 kilometers away! With this new knowledge, I asked him to refuse the delivery when it finally arrived. Have it sent back to the United States, and charge them to the hilt! To add insult to injury, the cab driver (who had not been paid) departed from his long wait without warning. Back inside cargo, I asked if someone would please call a taxi to take me back into town. The cab arrived twenty minutes later, and by about 5:00 p.m., I was back at the hotel, thinking about what had just taken place. It was all I could do to stop myself from calling LP Studio and ripping them a new one.

With nowhere else to turn, I took a walk up the block to Corte Ingles (the largest department chain in Spain). I figured, *I have nothing to lose. Let me look around and see what pops up.* Much to my shock and happiness, the staff at Corte Ingles was very knowledgeable concerning conversions, and electronics in general. With the assistance of my new best friend, Pedro, I was able to secure a series of adaptors for a Spanish power cord. We needed a total of five converters: three for the wall power source, and two for the power to the bass amp. For a total of thirty Euros, I seemed to have everything I needed! Filled with renewed energy and joy, I ran back to the hotel with my invention. The director of the jazz ensemble looked at me in awe. It felt good. We put the gadgets all together, said a short prayer (which for me included never cursing again if it worked), and flipped the switch to the on position. It worked! I nearly had a stroke! After roughly two hundred Euros spent on taxi rides and hours of wasted time at the airport and cargo, the end result was a mere thirty Euros spent at the local chain store.

It was now about 6:30 p.m., and I realized it was time to leave for our concert venue. My able guides gathered all the performers. We boarded our buses for the short ride and arrived at the concert site. Upon arrival, I ran inside to further prepare the stage and make sure the dressing rooms were unlocked. During this time, the instrumentalists were beginning to set up their individual instruments. As I was making my rounds, I noticed the bassist was setting up his amplifier. I caught him out of the corner of my eye as he plugged in the amplifier. It was something out of a horror film, where you see a person walking into a very dangerous situation and you start yelling at the screen, "No, no, don't go in there!" As I was getting the first words out of my mouth, "No! Don't—" I couldn't get out "turn it on!" The youngster turned on the power source without attaching all the converters properly. He shorted the amplifier out, and it was rendered useless.

Like the commercial says: 704 dollars for the rental of the amplifiers, 200 Euros for taxis, 30 Euros for power cords and converters. An eager young man wanting to play his bass: priceless!

CHAPTER 27

The State of New Jersey vs. Arts Alive

"If you can't lower heaven, raise hell."

—Mother Jones

I shared several e-mails with Chuck explaining how my production company was under attack from the State of New Jersey Department of Taxation. Chuck's style of writing back was if we were having an open dialog, not a narrative.

February 13, 2005
Arts Alive is doing reasonably well, despite all of the BS a small business goes through. I have some of that BS to share with you now. AAI has been hit with one heck of a disability bill from the State of New Jersey. It seems that when I sent out the 1099s to my subcontractors, the state decided they should get in on the action. They have charged a penalty of $1.61 per $100 paid out to my "employees." Arts Alive filtered out nearly $100,000 this season—you do the math. Needless to say, I am having a cash flow problem.

Good God, that is a disaster. Can you pay it off to the state over time? Is this the first time that they whacked you, and will they look to the past? Have you talked with an accountant? If not, you probably should.

The five-figure bill is due by February 24, so if you know of a bank that I can knock off in the next three weeks, send me the address.

Not funny. I would require a change of underwear at this point.

On the flip side, AAI is upping its usual number of bookings this season. I have taken on eight more concerts at Carnegie Hall, and four more at Lincoln Center, the Pro Arte Chorale, Ars Musica, the New Philharmonic, the Morristown Choral Society, and a few others. See, even with the enormous bill facing me, I still am clinging to my carefree approach. It's only money, right?

Nice attitude, but you are full of crap!

Has it been nearly two months since I wrote? Is that possible? I guess time is everything … For instance, when it comes to paying taxes, regardless of when you may have screwed up—or *if* you even screwed up—the state of New Jersey will catch up to you eventually. Are you up for a good challenge? I could use your help and advice. (I am always calling on you in times of distress. Will you ever get sick of me?)

Unlikely.

Another chapter of my book is writing itself: The State of New Jersey vs. Arts Alive.

Back in September, I received a letter from the state of New Jersey that I was one of the lucky recipients of an audit. I turned the letter over to my well-paid accountant, who assured me that everything was in order. On the day of the audit, while I was at work with the NJSO, my cell phone rang. My accountant reported to me that everything seemed to be in order, and the auditor had departed with all the information needed. Little did we know that I would receive a letter in February that I owed the state nearly ten thousand dollars for back taxes for the 2002 and 2003 calendar years! I nearly went in my pants. What the heck was going on? I always filed on time, paid all fees owed, and kept meticulous business records.

The state was claiming that all those who worked for Arts Alive during this period were my employees, not independent contractors. If they were my employees, then I owed the appropriate taxes for each paycheck written. Along with the outstanding taxes, a surcharge, interest, and penalties were levied against my little company. My immediate thought was to string up my accountant. I called him, and we spoke about what was happening. Again I was reassured that he had filed correctly for each year in question. Still not satisfied or comforted by my accountant, I did some of my own research. I was able to read an article on the New Jersey State website regarding specific points on determining who is an employee and who is an independent contractor. There were twenty-two points that we needed to consider. Six points are clearly in my favor, three are clearly in favor of the state, and the remainders are all in the famous gray area. So what am I to do? On Friday, February 24, the due date, we called the auditor and informed him that we would not pay these fees. We further explained that we felt we had a strong case against the state. The auditor was taken aback, because most people roll over and pay the piper. He granted me an extension to prove our case before he placed the matter in the hands of his supervisor. The extension he granted us is March 4. That gives me one week to build a case. Chuck, this is unreal!

One hundred ninety-seven people received payment from Arts Alive during this period. Some got as little as $200, and others were paid as much as $8,500. If I asked my accountant to build the case with me, the cost would be enormous. For that reason, I have taken the task on full-time. I have the next six days to make things happen. I must show the state that each and every person listed in their files worked for other contractors. First step: contact the 180-plus musicians via e-mail and explain my situation.

Step 1: I wrote a short form letter, making it easy for each musician to respond to me in less than five minutes. I asked each musician to fill in their own name and add some other places of employment. Many included resumes, other non-musical jobs, and more. This will show the state that these folks work for many organizations. Below is a sample of an answered e-mail. I am told that the e-mails are legal because they states the date and time—something I cannot alter.

> In a message dated 2/25/05 3:15:13 p.m. Eastern Standard Time, jimneglia writes:

> I, Mr. "X," work for Arts Alive on a per-service basis. Arts Alive does not supply any instruments for my performance duties; I provide my own. Arts Alive is not responsible for providing a place to work, practice rooms, or warm-up locations. I work for Arts Alive as an independent contractor. Arts Alive has provided

me with a 1099 tax form when my income has exceeded $600 during a complete calendar year. In addition to my freelance work with Arts Alive, I work for several other orchestras and organizations; below is a list: New Philharmonic, Morristown, New Jersey, The Colonial Symphony, Morristown, New Jersey, The Westfield Symphony, Westfield, New Jersey, The Papermill Playhouse, Millburn, New Jersey, The State Opera, etc.

Signed:
Mr. X
20 Frankly Drive
This Is Crap, New Jersey 07068

You can see how important it is to prove that these musicians work for other organizations.

In addition to this nonsense, I have letters coming in from the local musicians union, as well as the American Federation of Musicians, explaining the steps a contractor or contracting company must follow. They state that Arts Alive must deduct work dues and make pension and health contributions on behalf of the client or organization hosting a particular event. This gets very sticky, because the state has been looking at my checkbook and clearly sees that I have made various (thousands of dollars) payments to the AFM pension fund, and so on. They feel if I am paying pension and health contributions, as well as deducting work dues, I am definitely the employer.

I am also in the process of writing a detailed explanation of what I actually do, and how it works in the music world. Starting idea: Please feel free to add, take away, etc.

> Arts Alive is a per-service music production company. The following procedure takes place from start to finish for each project (concert). This is how Arts Alive was operating during 2002 and 2003.

1. A client contacts Arts Alive. The client asks Arts Alive to *hire* [better: "*provide*"] musicians for a given event. Generally, the event consists of a rehearsal and a performance.

2. Arts Alive produces a budget for the event [*"and submits it to the client." What are the line items on the budget? Submit one to the IRS as an example.)*

3. Upon the client accepting the budget, Arts Alive sets about hiring the musicians as required and specified by the client. Arts Alive will pay the musicians.

4. Arts Alive contacts the appropriate musicians and asks if they are *[available and willing]* to perform the services requested. Arts Alive has no control of any sort over any of the musicians that it asks to play any job. If the musician has another job for the same time, or if the musician simply does not like the job, or if the musician would rather take time off to do nothing, Arts Alive has no control whatsoever over these matters. The musicians are independent of Arts Alive. Arts Alive does not book performance locations, rehearsal locations, or warm-up rooms. Arts Alive does not provide any musician with the instruments needed for the services. Arts Alive does not provide the necessary music scores, transportation, music stands, music stand lights, lighting, parking, food, or anything else to the musicians. *[Any insurance involved?]*

5. The client writes a check to Arts Alive to pay for the event: the musicians' fees, a fee for the service provided by Arts Alive, and the required AFM (American Federation of Musicians) union fees (see 6, 7 below).

6. Governing Arts Alive is the AFM (American Federation of Musicians). *[Better: AFM requirements are binding on Arts Alive because all of the musicians are AFM (American Federation of Musicians) members.]* The AFM requires Arts Alive to deduct work dues and send the funds to the Local Musicians Union. These work dues are based on each musician's wage for the services performed. Under the bylaws of the AFM, Arts Alive *must* write one check for union dues. Therefore, the deduction is made from the musicians' gross salary. One check is sent to the local union, together with a list of names of the musicians who participated in the service. With this dues check, a "V" or "W" contract is filed, listing all the names of the musicians who performed;

ensuring that proper credit is given to each participating player. *[Should you explain the V and the W contracts?]* Musicians are *not* permitted to pay union dues on their own.

7. Pension and health contributions also are required by the union. The bylaws of the AFM (American Federation of Musicians) require that within ten business days of the performance, the contractor (Arts Alive) must make to the AFM one, single payment covering pension and health contributions for all of the involved musicians, accompanied by a list all of the independent contractor musicians involved.

   The pension/health contribution is made to AFM by Arts Alive. *[Add "on behalf of the client." Is it in any way included on the bill to the client, or can you include it, thus showing that you simply pass it on to the AFM and are reimbursed by the client? That is, can you show the musicians fees on the bill as in two parts.*

Net fees to the musicians	*$$*
+ AFM required fees	*$$*
Gross fee payable Arts Alive	*$$$$*

   That is the way the fees are built.]

   These funds are applied to the AFM accounts of the musicians who have provided their services for the event. Musicians are *not* permitted to make pension or health contributions on their own.

8. *All fees for salaries, union dues, pension, and health are paid by the client. Arts Alive is merely the facilitator of the transaction.*

Are you confused yet? I am, and I'm at a loss of what more I can possibly do. My complete goal is to pay the smallest fees to the state. I know I will have to pay something, because they will not roll over, either.

As for the future of Arts Alive? Obviously the days of 1099 tax forms are over. I will move to W2 immediately.

(Whoa! What does your accountant say about that?)

Another option is to hire a payroll service to pay the musicians, *if* I can afford to hire a payroll service (adding nearly 25 percent to each client's bill).

Not if you are saving $4,000 by dumping the disability/workman's comp.

I can drop my disability coverage and worker comp policy, saving Arts Alive about $4,000 per year.

The fact that you have workman's comp might weigh against you with the IRS; ask the accountants. But when I hire a painter to paint my house, he is an independent contractor, yet I maintain liability insurance on the premises just in case. These are things that the accountant should be able to answer.

Maybe this is a wakeup call, and it is time to close shop?

Look, it depends what the IRS does. If they go against you, then you have to sit down and figure out a few things—like can you figure out how to meet the IRS' requirements for independent contractor status for the musicians; if not, can you afford to operate profitably by meeting the IRS' statutory requirements? One way or the other.

Maybe it is all for the best.

Wait a minute—cool your jets.

When the dust settles and I see where everything is, I will make a decision; until then, I will fight the good fight and will not fold my hand for anyone!

Absolutely! Listen, the IRS is a vile organization. They are interested to no degree in what is right—they just want your money. I had a run-in with them about the same issue at Mannes, in a somewhat different vein, in '78 or '79. You also will have to decide how far you can afford to push the case.

They really stink. I had one agent once who told me not to bother with right or wrong; he said that I should save them and myself the aggravation of fighting their claim—which was absolutely false—pay him what he wants, and then claim tax credit with New Jersey! The difference would be negligible. Son of a bitch! If worse came to worst, how would that apply to you, or would it at all?

And FYI, if I decide to file for bankruptcy, I, James Neglia, am responsible for all payroll taxes from past and present years. The S corporation status does not relieve me of those fees. Not now, not ever.

Yes, I know. But you are not there yet, and even with the filthy IRS, if worse comes to worst, you will be able to pay it off over time, and it will help you to save something by trading the payroll service for the disability insurance, even if you have to pass some on to the clients to remain competitive.

There is much to share about the NJSO. However, I am exhausted and am struggling to keep my eyes open. In a word, Järvi is truly amazing; great concerts this week, great music making. *This* is what keeps me sane, make no mistake about it.

Okay, keep your head up and be tough but not snotty. Keep me informed, okay? Happiness, even under trying circumstances.

A follow-up e-mail a few weeks later:

The audit is over. I have settled all matters with the state. After countless hours of talks with the auditor, we agreed on the following: I will pay 25 percent of the total amount levied against my business, or $2,450. I will consider all musicians who work for Arts Alive employees. In return, the state of New Jersey will sign a waiver preventing any audit concerning Arts Alive during the 2004 calendar year. This was the best deal I could manage, considering.

If the state were to audit me for 2004, I would surely be found guilty of the same charge. In 2004, AAI had its most productive year, and I would have been up a creek without a paddle. Perhaps an additional four or five thousand is saved. Anyway, I am not discouraged by all this nonsense. I am picking up where I left off and looking to a brighter future.

I am not sure if I told you, but as of February 18, all musicians are being issued W4 forms, and most if not all of my clients have agreed to pick up the fees in order to keep working with me—another blessing. I have decided to process all payrolls myself; it is the most cost-effective way to operate. I will need to pay all fees (unemployment, disability, etc.) monthly. My accountant is going to show me how I can do this on my own online. All forms are on the Web at my disposal; all I need to do is write a check.

I would place this entire fiasco in the category of "growing pains." I can deal with that; I will *not* close my doors, and I will emerge stronger than before.

A million sincere thanks for all your help with my presentation to the state. You are truly part of my support system.

In the summer of 2005, just four months after the audit, I decided that the efforts and energy of running and maintaining my small business were not worth the amount of work and money it took to keep it going. The final insult was paying another one thousand dollars to the state of New Jersey to dissolve my business and incorporated status. I was incredibly sad to do this, but I knew in the long run, it was for my own protection, if not sanity.

All these years later, I know I made the right decision in 2005. As the music business goes, many of the organizations I was working for back then have filed chapter eleven bankruptcy. They closed their doors due to lack of funding efforts or simply a lack of interest. I have retained a few of my long-time clients, happy to work with them all these years.

With the closing of Arts Alive, I felt part of my past coming full circle. The startup money used to begin the company came from a *very* small inheritance I had received upon my mother's passing in 1998. I wanted to find some way to have her memory live on. I took the few dollars realized and pumped it into incorporating a name, purchasing stationery, securing a toll-free phone number, opening a business account, and putting the remainder into that business account to pay the first few months' bills.

The business actually turned a profit every year it was in existence. Projects here in New Jersey, New York, Pennsylvania, Connecticut, and finally Europe all made it possible to sustain my small business. Through my contacts over the years, I was able to co-produce a number of musical events in the Czech Republic, Slovak Republic, Austria, Poland, and Hungary, really placing Arts Alive on the international map.

CHAPTER 28

Take Me Home

In the spring of 2005, my life continued its upward path when Sasha came into my life. Although we had been working together at the symphony for many years, it wasn't until then that we took the next step. With committed focus we joined together as one and began our new journey. She brought me many reasons to rejoice, but two of the best were her sons, Phillip and Daniel.

December 4, 2007:

Dear Chuck,

The Sunday after Thanksgiving, Sasha and I were visiting my brother and his family in East Hanover. After a filling dinner, we decided to go for a walk to help jump-start our metabolism. While walking, we stumbled on a "For Sale" sign sitting in front of this beautiful quasi-Victorian-style home. We debated the price and decided to call the realtor to find out who was closer to the seller's asking price. We rang the number on the sign, but there was no answer. We left a message, hung up the phone, and continued on our way. A few hours later, while on our way home to Brooklyn, my cell phone rang. Kristine, the realtor, introduced herself and quickly began to tell us about the house. She told us about the layout and all the assorted particulars, which included four bathrooms and a full apartment in the basement. The description of the house sounded great, and we asked her to set up an appointment for us to see for ourselves. The earliest time we could all get together was the following Sunday, December 2, before our 3:00 p.m. performance (Mahler 2). Sasha's parents were coming to that particular performance, so without choice, they were with us when we went to see the house.

At the appointed time, we pulled up to the house and parked in the spacious driveway. As we got out of the car, we couldn't help but feel we had arrived at a very comfortable place. When we walked through the front door, the comfort and vibe were incredibly strong. I wasn't sure exactly what it was about the house, but we could feel it all around us. The layout was as I'd pictured from the conversation with Kristine. The house was built in 1989, and the builder was also the seller. The structure was sound, the house well maintained.

During the walk-through, we discovered the vibe. It was hidden in the basement. We descended the basement stairs into a large apartment, fully equipped with a full kitchen and a fourth bathroom. However, the apartment was set up as a recording studio, housing a full set of drums, guitars, basses, mixing boards, amplifiers, microphones—the works. Around the corner from the kitchen was a soundproof fourteen feet by fourteen feet recording room, which I would use as a studio for my own drum set. Can you imagine? Next to the studio was a full bathroom and hook-up for a washer and dryer. Additionally, there was a separate entrance to the apartment below the house.

Aside from the basement apartment, there are four large bedrooms on the second floor, along with two full bathrooms. The master bath has two separate rooms, one for the Jacuzzi and shower, and one for the sink and commode. The second bathroom is big enough to place a couch in it—unreal. On top of all that, there is a room that is well-lit by natural light, and shelving is already installed; a perfect office.

The first floor has a very large kitchen with all new appliances (that stainless stuff—Sasha was in her glory), dining room, laundry room, half bath, and a thirty feet by fifteen feet family room with a fireplace. At the back of the family room, there are three large French doors leading out to the above-ground twelve feet by twenty-five feet deck.

After walking around the house for about twenty minutes, Sasha's father Marik came to me and said in very broken English and Russian, "Jim, please find a way to live here."

In one word: wow! Unbelievable! (That's two words, isn't it …) This is amazing—that the whole thing happened in a totally positive karma. And on top, your in-laws are enthusiastic.

This was an amazing show of support. I never imagined they would want their daughter and grandchildren to move away from Brooklyn. Zhanna (Sasha's mother) speaks better English, and she added many comments recognizing the opportunity the kids would have being in such a place. How good this home would be for Sasha and the vast amount of room in which we would have to live and work. We spoke to the realtor about the school system to get a better sense of the town; she commented with all good remarks. Another plus: the house is about fifteen minutes up Route 280 from the NJPAC, an easy commute, and there are no tolls.

Now, I tell you, Chuck, we weren't really looking to move, but fate played a hand in this decision, and we purchased the house less than twenty-four hours later.

By the way, Sasha was closer on the price than I was. In a matter of three weeks, we secured a mortgage, made it through attorney review, passed all appraisals from the mortgage folks, and had our own house inspection completed. We are now in holding mode, waiting for all the pieces to fall into place. The contract reads "February 15 or before" for our closing, but the sellers would like to speed things up, and we are happy to comply.

We are keeping the condo in Brooklyn and will rent it out. Price-wise, we can either break even on the rent or make a few dollars. Time will tell. We just know it is not time to sell here, but if we had to, of course we would do what we needed.

So there is the news and one other little offering: Sasha and I are getting married next Sunday, December 30, in a small ceremony at my brother's house. Just our immediate families will attend. So, any comments?

Are you kidding? Who could speak after all of this? Just amazing. Listen, you are a good guy, and you have always done the right thing—well, maybe once or twice you have skidded a little, but what the heck, who hasn't. And you have planned and worked hard, and you deserve all of this great stuff.

I don't have to tell you that I wish for you the best that there is, and it sounds as though you are on the way to exactly that.

To Chuck on Saturday, December 29, 2007
Well, it seems like I finally shocked, or shall I say, stunned you.

Well, maybe a little.

It only took me forty-four years and a little skidding here and there.

Everyone is entitled to a little skidding.

We are excited about tomorrow and our pending nuptials and what looks to be a wonderful family gathering.

No kidding? What a shock! If you didn't get excited about that, you would never get excited about __anything__!

Beyond that, we are hopeful for a January 28 house closing; I should have more news on Monday. You know, Chuck, this is an exciting time for us. I believe most people would be nervous or at the very least a bit shaky, but I feel like a rock.

A very good omen! Now, if I were twenty-three again and getting married or purchasing a home (never mind both), I am sure I would have soiled my pants, but the only thing I feel at this moment is complete happiness.

That, my friend, is the way that it is supposed to be.

Two thousand seven has been a magical year: Sasha, the boys, a new home, a great job, performing, Neeme extending his contract, a possible Broadway show, old dear friends, and so many other wonderful things. I guess the old saying is true: one does have to pass through hell in order to get to heaven.

Be grateful and enjoy it all!

Have things calmed down for your holidays? More visitors?

Well, the family contingent arrived with an eighteen-month-old, and he promptly got sick with an ear infection and infected everyone else. It's been a thrill a minute. Listen—I send my best wishes to you and Sasha for a wonderful day and an even more wonderful life together!

CHAPTER 29

Switzerland and Broadway

September 6 and 9, 2007
Good to hear from you again—I thought that you had fled to Patagonia!

Sorry for the delay in writing back to you. I have news for you, but first, in short our trip was simply sensational. You may want to grab a cup of coffee; this e-mail may turn out longer than I expected.

We did make a few diversions from our planned itinerary, which reflected our collective on-the-spot mood and weather conditions.

Makes sense.

The last two days in Geneva were dreary, wet and generally ugly to wake up to.

Geneva is okay, but to tell you the truth, it never knocked me out. The Mannes Orchestra played there on the 1995 tour.

As a result, each morning we pointed our car out of town; first to Annecy, which was one of the highlights of the trip!

I believe it—a beautiful place.

The day before we were set to fly to Amsterdam, we all woke up before 7:00 a.m. Seeing that the weather was being uncooperative, I gathered the troops, got in the car, and left town. My thought was to visit Chamonix, where the weather was perhaps drier. The greatest part of being in the Geneva area was that geographically, we were minutes from France, so off we went. As we were approaching the French frontier, the weather didn't seem to be getting any better. When we were in Freiberg, we also woke up to damp weather, but as we descended the mountain, we found ourselves enjoying seventy degrees and dry weather all week.

I assume that a good time was had by all.

Still in the rain, we continued through the eastern tip of France. In doing so, we noticed signs for Mont Blanc. For some reason, my mind couldn't figure out how that was at all possible (silly me). Following the E712 (signs for A40/E25/Chamonix-Mont-Blanc/Turin/Annemasse/Milan), we pressed on. Our breakfast stop came 120 kilometers later, in the beautiful village of Aosta, Italy. Aosta was about 130 kilometers from Geneva, just a stone's throw away.

Very good cheese from Aosta!

Mind you, because my wife is Russian, I have been learning and speaking for quite a few years now, so you can imagine how happy I was to hear my native Italian. Although very rusty, my memory did not fail me. I even managed to dazzle Sasha with my (little) expertise. We spent part of the day eating dry sausages, cheeses, breads in their abundance and sipping espresso.

Could be worse!

The drive to Aosta took us through Mont Blanc (now forty Euros round trip) and from sixteen degrees Celsius on the wet French side to a reasonably warm thirty-three on the Italian side. Sasha commented how all good things are Italian; I just laughed.

I believe that!

Finally, after hours and hours of sitting and happily relaxing in the same four-square-block radius, we knew we had to begin our journey back to our hotel. It was getting late, and we needed about two hours to find our way back to Geneva. We also had scheduled a 4:30 a.m. wakeup call so we could make our 7:00 a.m. flight back to Amsterdam. Once back on the highway (which was pristine), we headed back toward the eleven-kilometer Mont Blanc tunnel. We marveled at the mandatory distance between cars *and* that everyone obeyed the laws!

Too dangerous not to.

Somewhat tired from waking so early in the morning, along with the day's travel, we made our way slowly but surely back to Switzerland. Although we were tired, a jolt of energy hit us when we saw signs for Chamonix. And you know what I did, don't you? You got it: I took the exit and snaked down the mountain until the narrow road opened up into a beautiful little village stuck on the side of the mountainside. By this time, we were completely energized by our new surroundings. We spent the next few hours milling about, looking, seeing, and gasping from the wealth of beauty around us. Chamonix is near the massive peaks of the Aiguilles Rouges. Chamonix shares the summit of Mont Blanc with its neighboring community of Courmayeur in Italy. You can imagine the amazing view we had, even during the evening.

All our senses were invigorated. Breathing the fresh, cool air turned up our digestive tract, and the corner restaurant boasted the best firewood meal in town. We couldn't resist. We enjoyed a meal that included a double offering of escargot, white fish, and meat tidbits, which we would actually cook at our table on a portable wood grill. And what is a good meal if it isn't accompanied by the most perfect bottle of red wine? We ordered a light bottle to drink with our most perfect meal. Afterward, we roamed the streets for nearly an hour more, taking in the architecture and feeling of this remote hideaway. In a word, stunning.

By 11:00 p.m. we knew we needed to begin our journey back to Geneva. The first thirty minutes of our trip back was difficult, as we were snaking back up the mountainside; two narrow lanes, half guard rails, and exhausted and full-bellied passengers. Phillip was half asleep, but my wonderful partner talked with me the entire trip back.

I always wanted to see that town, but I never made it. Sounds as though I really missed something!

We covered over 1,800 kilometers during our too-short, 11-day stay. Every mile was filled with the most extreme beauty I have ever experienced in my life. I have traveled extensively over the past twenty years (including the Austrian Alps, Salzburg, Innsbruck, and more), but nothing parallels this part of the world. Perhaps it was our choice of smaller cities and villages, or perhaps the disposition of our dear Swiss? Who knows, but it all worked for us.

(*Well, good. The Swiss do not have too savory a history, especially since 1939—and if it wasn't for the scenery, what would they have after one thousand years of history? A cuckoo clock, a chocolate bar, and a numbered bank account.*

Now, on to the news. About three weeks before we left for Europe, an old project resurfaced. I am not sure if I ever wrote to you about a musical called *A Tale of Two Cities*, based on the Dickens novel?

Yes, you did. Quite a bit, in fact. I assumed that it had just died.

In August 2004, I became involved with a twenty-nine-hour production and reading of the musical *A Tale of Two Cities* at the Little Schubert Theater in Manhattan. At the time, I was hired only to play timpani and percussion, but that quickly changed. When the producers learned that I was the personnel manager of the NJSO, they called me and asked if I would take care of their musical needs, which included percussion and timpani rentals, three synthesizer rentals with programming fees, locations to rehearse, and the actual hiring of all personnel. Of course I agreed to do this work. I began by diligently researching the best prices I could for all concerned. Things were coming together nicely, and I was able to cash in on some favors owed to me over the years.

As the reading approached, so did the union problems. It was at this time that I began negotiations with the theatre department of Local 802. The executive producers of the show gave me approval to work out the best deal I could in order for us to move forward. We had a limited budget that I had to stretch to cover all musicians and rental fees. There simply wasn't enough money to hire nineteen musicians, pay health and pension, rent a rehearsal space and synthesizers, and pay a programmer. However, I began to see the way, and after three days of negotiating, the final deal was signed. Each musician would be paid a nominal fee for all twenty-nine hours.

However, what they got in return was first right of refusal if the show ever opened on Broadway.

Good idea.

I assembled an amazing band of both orchestral-trained and Broadway-sharp pros. The band kicked ass, and all were happy with my efforts. The project was completed as scheduled, I came in just under budget, the show was magnificent, and life went on.

Okay. Well done. I am not surprised.

Now and again, there was some talk about raising the money required for a possible Broadway opening. It all sounded great, but my mind was on Arts Alive and the NJSO.

Fast forward to July 2007. While in Switzerland, I received a call from the producers. The money had been raised to begin productions. We were set to open on October 13 at the Asolo Theater in Sarasota, with talks about a possible Broadway opening in the spring of 2008. The big man, Don Frantz, the general manager of Town Square Productions, now had reservations about hiring me as music coordinator. I remembered that I had protected myself in the 2004 negotiations. I named myself music coordinator in the Little Schubert Theater contract. At the time, one of the only reasons the union agreed to the substantially lower rate was because they had been working with me for years. I had assured them that I would be on board for all future *Tale* projects.

I understood Don's apprehensions. I knew he was accustomed to working with seasoned professionals in the field, but there was no way I was going to back down. After a very long phone conversation with Don, I made him the following offer: Don't pay me for two weeks. At the end of that time, we can look at all I had done, and if he was satisfied he had the right guy for the job, he could sign me up. If he decided to use me, then he would pay me retroactive to my actual starting date. He agreed, and I felt vindicated.

It wasn't until a much later time that I learned more about why he was so concerned. He had been working on an enormous project in Beijing for the past few years, and he was spending more time there than here.

It was when I heard this that I understood why he wanted to go with his other people. He really didn't want to worry about any of the higher positions attached with *Tale,* because he wasn't here personally to oversee everything most of the time.

A day or so after our conversation, he sent me a detailed e-mail on what he needed done. I had never seen, heard, or dealt with many of the issues he was presenting, but I began to do my homework. Within a few days I had answered all his questions with success and in detail. This was the last time I heard from Don for several weeks.

It was time to take my holidays, and for my wife and I to leave for Europe. I sent Don an email with my itinerary. I charged my Blackberry, and boarded the plane for Geneva. A few days into the trip, my Blackberry was ringing or buzzing off the hook! Laurie, Don's very able associate general manager, was requesting immediate relief in the form of my help. I think I ignored the first dozen calls and e-mails because by this time, I still had no signed contract. Finally, I called her from Europe and told her that I was here to help, but I had already done more work than I felt comfortable doing without a firm offer or deal.

Absolutely right! Work without profit is slavery. And the most important ass in the world is your own, and it has to be covered first and best.

She replied "We need you, and I'm sending your contract immediately." After a couple of minor rewrites, I officially signed my contract. We worked via e-mail and hotel fax. All this excitement while on my much-needed holidays.

Good for you. She ain't no dummy, either.

Don't ask how I am going to manage both the NJSO and *Tale.* Time will tell how things will work out, but in the meantime, I am rocking along and enjoying the pre-production aspects of a show. I am learning, understanding, and working toward my newly expanded functions. I am beginning to understand more acutely the needs of those I am now supervising. I am responsible for maintaining and driving the orchestrators, copyists, music director, synthesizer programmers, and all who are involved in the pre-production in the music department. As far as the hectic pace, comparing it to the NJSO, it is like a bullet being shot out of a high-powered pistol. The NJSO is more like a tired elephant moving toward a good night's sleep.

Okay, great. Terrific opportunity, and it sounds as though you handled it well. But you know what I am about to say. Can you ride one tired elephant at the same time that you are riding a bullet fired from a high-powered pistol? There are a zillion risks involved here, but I guess that they all boil down into one, and that is: are you jeopardizing your terrific job with the NJSO?

Things are moving so fast, I can't even keep up with my own note-taking. I guess I could use an assistant these days.

Yeah, but you ain't got one, and it ain't a-gonna get easier as time goes on.

There is so much happening, so many changes these past few years, so many opportunities plopping on my lap. You know something? It feels good. Sending my very best to you.

I'll bet! And you know that I am sending my best to you! Be calm and cool!

Promise to keep in touch.

No question, and keep me informed on how it all is rocking along.

September 11, 2007
A few facts I missed but you caught (no big surprise there). The original nineteen-piece orchestra has been reduced to eleven for the Asolo production, among them, three fully programmed synthesizers. However, when we return to New York City, the plan is to increase from the original nineteen to possibly twenty-four. I do believe this will happen, as the producers have built up the theater representatives (those who want the show in their house) into believing so and budgeting accordingly.

Sounds okay.

I have no knowledge if Don has fully accepted me as his music coordinator, although through countless e-mails and phone conversations with Laurie, I am certain that she is pleased. In turn, she will keep Don informed. Laurie is a no-nonsense, straight-shooting machine-gun of a person. She is as strong as a bull, and I love it, and I love working with her. In the short time I have been working on this project, she has sung my praises on several occasions; so far so good. She must be in regular touch with Don despite his being in China.

Let's hope so.

NJSO and *Tale*: At this stage of the game, I will have completed all pre-production on *Tale* by October 8. After that, I sit back and wait to see how the critics feel about the show. The NJSO season begins on October 9 (what luck!). I have been preparing for the season, and no one in the office, including my general manager, has any reason to believe that I am not functioning at 100 percent. I am no dummy; I will not risk a job that offers me a steady paycheck, along with my medical and pension, for a Broadway show, ever. I am aware that the show could open and close in the same week, or month, or year. Make no mistake about it; it will close, and I will still be at the NJSO.

Listen, I know that you are a professional and a very smart and sharp one at that, but I would guess that there still are elements of risk in this for you—relative to the NJSO. I assume that they do not know that you are involved in this—right?

My real problem can come when the show opens in New York. But at this stage, why should I concern myself with this enormous unknown variable of *when?* The show may open in April or later, perhaps as late as September 2008. If it's April, that may be trickier than September, but I will figure this out in time, as needed.

I hope so.

Life is funny. One day Pittsburgh wants me, and the next I am hoping Town Square Productions wants me. If all goes well with the pre-production and my specific duties, my hope is that Don will rehire me for the next project, then the next and the next one after that. He took another person under his wing about fifteen years ago, gave him his first show, and never let him go. Now he has nine shows running on Broadway, collecting a weekly check on each.

Well, of course, you never can know what things will lead to, but for God's sake—take care of your day job.

The agreement: before signing, I consulted Local 802 for advice. I was informed that most items met their approval; what didn't, we amended and renegotiated. Local 802 reassured me that it was a standard deal, and even if certain demands weren't okay with me, I should sign the contract.

It looks like I will be in Sarasota from September 30 through October 8. Along with the large daily per-day salary, I will receive a per diem for housing and travel. This is above and beyond the more than adequate startup fee. Always thinking to press forward, onward and upward I go! Thanks a million for reading my ranting and getting back to me. More to follow.

You don't rant, and I am happy to do it. Good luck! Looking forward.

September 30, 2007:
Chuck, Just a quick note. I am leaving for Sarasota tomorrow evening. I will keep notes and keep you up to date with things.

Okay. Best of luck. Just remember, you know exactly what has to be done and how to do it—and you have very good instincts! In bocca al lupo!

I am not too concerned right now; my eyes are on my day gig, I promise you, but I am sure questions will arise.

Tell me, if you were not in Sarasota, what would you be doing for the NJSO? Are you taking this as vacation time or a leave, or what?

You know, Chuck, I cannot worry about what might happen, either at the NJSO or *Tale*.

The hell you can't—what are the possibilities? Figure them out and prepare for them in advance.

So far things have worked out, and perhaps things will continue to work out in the future; time will tell. I will be in touch.

Of course—hope for the best but prepare for the worst.)

October 31, 2007
Well? What happened?

October 31, 2007

So much has happened in these past weeks. Let me start by saying that the show is a complete success. The reviews of the opening have been extremely positive and rewarding. Those above me have congratulated me and accepted me as a person filled with energy, drive, dedication, and a type-A personality. I fit right in! I am so very happy.

Since I last wrote, my schedule has been tedious, to say the least. I stayed in Sarasota up until the last conceivable second before the NJSO season started on October 9. Once the season started and up until this past Sunday, I traveled back and forth to Florida a total of nine times. I worked out my schedule to get on a 1:45 p.m. flight from Newark International right after our 12:30 p.m. NJSO ending rehearsal time. I would arrive in Sarasota by 5:00 p.m. and work until my 6:05 a.m. flight the next morning. I napped on the flight home and went directly from Newark airport to my 10:00 a.m. NJSO rehearsal at the NJPAC the same morning. Yes, it was insane, but necessary. At least once I recall staying awake for more than twenty-four hours. Chuck, looking back, I can honestly tell you there has not been one moment where either job has suffered the stresses of the other.

I know I am not superhuman, and I am blatantly aware that I could not keep up such a schedule for a prolonged period of time. I knew there was a finite amount of time I needed to sustain such insanity. I just pushed until the show's double opening happened on October 26 and 27. Yup, we had two openings! One for London and one for Paris (charged double ticket price for each with a large party afterward, which included catered food from both cities). I could not make it down for the London opening, but I made my final journey (hopefully) for the Paris opening. Watching the show, I was moved to tears during the first act several times. Perhaps these were tears of exhaustion, but I would like to think it was coupled with the work we accomplished during the month. We produced one of the most moving and captivating shows in recent theater history. Yes, I am proud, *extremely* proud, of our collective hard work. It was worth every minute of lost sleep, dedication, direction, and supervision I had in my being.

The Asolo Theater seats five hundred, and we have now sold out every performance through the closing on November 18. The buzz here is that the news of our success will find its way up north to all the deep-pocket investors. We speculate that the New York theater folks should be fighting for us to open in their home.

I admit life in Florida was difficult. My musical problems ranged from irresponsible music supervision to an inept copyist team who was working around the clock just to catch up. During the past month, I needed to fire several key people in the music department. One key person was the copyist and his entire team; this was painful but necessary. After the firing, I needed to replace the team with a new staff immediately. Within six hours I had secured a top-notch replacement from New York. We negotiated a substantial contract, and I had him and his team on the next flight to Sarasota before nightfall. Funny—there is nothing money can't solve! On the positive side, the orchestrations are brilliant. Our orchestra of eleven (led by the genius Ed Kessel) sounded like a full symphonic orchestra. Ed knows how to build the orchestral sound to the maximum; he has shown his complete understanding of all that he needed to convey. The breakdown of each instrumentalist was used to its maximum. Bravo, Ed!

The show was moving at such speed that I had difficulty keeping up with daily events. If you compare the *Tale* pace with my life at the symphony, your head would spin at the amount of sheer energy required. That is not to say my work at the NJSO isn't equally important or demanding, but it's definitely different. The show has helped me put and keep things in perspective. I have a new approach to my orchestra life and the challenges I deal with on a daily basis. I am settled and things are good.

If Town Square Productions honored me with another opportunity to work as music coordinator on one of their upcoming musicals, I would jump on it. I have been motivated beyond my own expectations. There were times when I felt I was a freshman in college again: new surroundings, new topics, new faces, new problems. But somehow it was all familiar. This has been an amazing journey, which I would be happy repeating.

I am nearly certain that *A Tale of Two Cities* will open on Broadway within six months. If so, this will be a recipe for disaster. I cannot see how it would be possible to do both—not again, not on Broadway. If fate is on my side, we will delay until the summer. Only time will have the answer to that all-important question.

I am preparing myself for whatever comes—NJSO, Broadway, perhaps a new direction is in store for me. If you would have asked me what I was going to be doing at this time one year ago, the answer would have been clear. These days, I make no promises.

November 3, 2007
Wow! Absolutely unbelievable! I don't mean the show—I mean you! I can't imagine how you managed to bring this off without exploding or coming apart in pieces. But I can imagine the amount of energy and sacrifice and skill required. You are a juggler! Did you need any anti-sleep drugs?

The fact that the show is an apparently terrific hit is a bonus; your personal accomplishment would have been just as amazing even if it flopped, which, grazie a dio, it didn't. Interesting enough, the whole business provided you with a showcase for a whole variety of your management skills, which you demonstrated to great advantage. Bravo!

Old adage: If two things can happen, the one that's the worst will be the one. Bad break with the NJSO flutist in Sarasota, but as the man said, "stuff" happens. The thing now is to prepare for the inevitable questions that will come at you sooner or later from NJSO management. You can pretty well guess what they will have to say, so get the answers set up. Am I wrong, or is your long suit that whatever you did was okay, because things ran just fine at the orchestra?

You're right—maybe a new direction, but be calm. One drop is not an ocean. The next few weeks should be interesting. What will happen if the show does open in New York during the NJSO season?

Great Job, Jimmie. Happiness!

November 3, 2007
I managed to pull things off by being as prepared as I could be pre-NJSO season. By the middle of September, I had hired nearly all the extra musicians needed through the end of December (our first break). With that done, I was able to focus on *Tale* with more than my normal energy. Although I spent a few days near exhaustion, the new challenge revived

me every time. No sleeping drugs were required, although a nightly glass or two of the red grape helped me find my way to a deep sleep.

The production team seemed to be satisfied with my work, as was the big man, Don Frantz. I cannot predict the future, but I would not be surprised to be working for him again sometime. As *Tale* progresses to Broadway, I will need to pick up where I left off in Sarasota, but this time without the flights. Once I get the green light, I can begin filing contracts, securing an orchestra, and putting more key people in place. After that, there is basically nothing else to do. I have a friend who is a music coordinator for multiple shows. His advice to me is to always surround myself with the best people. No kidding. This will ensure the success of the show and increase my personal longevity.

I may have a lot to consider, but not just yet. I do agree with you when you say one drop does not make an ocean. This is why I am calmly dealing with the *possibility* of a successful show and future with Town Square Productions. Who would have thought, all those years ago, that I would have any management skills? There must be a parallel between those skills, my percussion dedication, and your office.

I will stay in touch. Your words, thoughts, and input are always welcome. Chuck, you are a balancing force in my life, and a person whom I respect, admire, love, and will continue to look to for guidance and advice. So stick around!

CHAPTER 30

Final Correspondence

March 13, 2007
My Dear Friend,

Writing is one way I truly love to correspond, but to hear your voice on the other end of my receiver last week was incredibly rewarding. I am glad I called and was able to hear your voice and get an update. We were on our way to our symphony performance when you came into my mind so strongly. At that very moment, I told my wife how strong the feeling was that I had to call you. She said, "Call now, right now. Don't wait for later or tomorrow." Good advice! So I picked up the phone and hit "Ray" in my phone memory bank. You are the only Ray in my book. The phone rang and you picked up. I was happy to have found you home and that we were able to share a few minutes together talking.

To be honest, I am worried about you. I know you are dealing with Margie and all that entails. I cannot even imagine what you are feeling or experiencing. All I can say is I am here for you anytime you need. Just pick up the phone, and we can chat away at a moment's notice.

I am thrilled to have received your warm letter of March 3. I am happy you had the energy and focus to write and fill me in on more details of your daily life. What is this about hip surgery? I had no idea. I trust you have fully recovered, or are at least close to meeting that challenge. I don't like thinking of you alone in Kerrville. I know you are incredibly strong and have the support of so many—your children, friends, parishioners, and distant New Jersey friend—but I ask you to please call as you feel the need.

Please write to me and tell me the doctor's interpretation of this silver dollar-size lump; I am most disturbed to hear this news. Perhaps a Kerrville visit is in order sooner rather than later. Please let me know what is happening with your health, as I cannot bear to think of you in any pain.

I don't mind your hand-written letters at all; it brings us full circle. This is how we began so many years ago.

Talk soon,
Jim

Before, during and after the March 2007 letter, I was immersed in a project that snatched up a great deal of my time. Although Ray and Margie were always in my thoughts, I rarely had the energy to dedicate the time for a thorough letter. My plan at the time was to continue documenting my current activities. These included opening a musical production of *A Tale of Two Cities* at the Asolo Theater in Sarasota Florida, and later our opening on Broadway in New York City. Needless to say, I had a very busy few years and I worked feverishly on the show, all the while maintaining my regular position with the Symphony. There wasn't enough time in the day to work both jobs, raise the kids, and be a husband, but somehow, I managed it with reasonably great success. Time simply was at a premium, but I still managed to keep detailed notes on the productions of *Tale*, and perhaps one day, I will publish them as well.

Often my thoughts drifted to Ray and Margie. I attempted to call Ray several times during this lost time, but I was never able to reach him. From the very start of our relationship, we had a sort of forbidden deal about using the phone. "Let's just write," was our motto. On occasion, the phone would ring either here in New Jersey or there in Texas. When my mother passed in 1998, the phone rang. When I learned of Margie's Alzheimer's disease, I called him. Some surgeries, detected lumps, and other medical conditions all warranted phone calls. Ray and I used the phone sparingly, but when we really felt the need for that immediate gratification, the phone was our chosen method of contact.

With my new positions in various organizations, I decided to get rid of my beeper, phone, Palm Pilot, and whatever other electronic devices I possessed. I gave them all up for one device: a Blackberry. In doing so, I was able to combine the multiple items I had into one, easy-to-use device. The one problem was that all my contacts were not as compatible as I thought they would be. In some cases—well, in most—I had the same person in my Blackberry with multiple listings. When I would perform a search for a person, I would usually use the first contact for them that came up, not paying too much attention to the next entries.

Fast forward to December 25, 2009. While updating the contacts in my Blackberry, I realized that I had two entries for Ray Benjamin. One entry had an area code of 803, and the other 830—an obvious typo on my part. My heart began to pound and pound, as if I had just figured out the great mystery of life. I had been calling and searching for Ray, scouring the Internet, calling Kerrville newspapers and hospitals, and no Ray. I dialed the number using area code 803. A few rings of the phone, and the same unfamiliar voice came on the annoying answering machine. I hung up, paused, and thought for a moment that I must have been dialing the wrong number for the past year. Indeed, I was.

I picked up the phone and dialed area code 830, and a few rings later, I was greeted by a warm, kind, questioning voice. "Who is this?"

I responded, "It is me, it is Jim from New Jersey! Is this the home of Ray and Margie Benjamin?"

"Yes, it is; let me get Ray for you." I was overjoyed to hear that Ray and Margie were alive and well.

During the course of our conversation, I learned that Margie was in an assisted living facility and was rapidly declining from her Alzheimer's disease. Ray sounded very weak, and with almost no spirit in his voice at all. I felt true, sincere pain and compassion for my friend from Texas. After hanging up the phone, I sat down and wrote a very long letter to Ray, summarizing the past twelve months of my life and all the new adventures that had taken place. After sending the letter, one month turned into two, and two turned into three. I had become so busy with work and family that I fell into the trap of life. During this horrible trap, I neglected to follow up on my lengthy letter. Nearly a year had passed before I wrote again.

It was December 2010. After mourning and suffering personally for nearly a year the loss of my brother, I was still stuck in the doldrums. I decided to pull myself together and go to the store, purchase Christmas cards, and send them out. I felt the need to reach out to all those friends and family members I had neglected over the past year. One of the first cards I wrote was to Ray. I wrote very few words but chose them carefully. Much to my surprise, about a week later, I received a response from him. The card was simple yet perfect.

> January 4, 2010
> Dear James,
>
> So glad to hear from you. You're still my favorite pen pal. I'm now living alone, as Margie passed on June 11. I'm adjusting; I went to five bereavement classes, and it helped me. There is a possibility that I may move to Colorado to be near my daughter. Hope you are well and having lots of music.
>
> As Ever,
> Ray

After receiving the card, which touched my very soul, I picked up the phone to speak with my friend. We spoke, and Ray sounded stronger than the last time we spoke a year earlier. We spoke of Margie, my brother, Christmas, moving to Colorado, life in Kerrville, the million-dollar entertainment center just built in his community, and much more. His closing words to me were, "This is the best Christmas present I could have wished for." Needless to say, I was moved beyond words and realized, once again, how blessed I was to have people like Ray in my life. By the end of the conversation, I learned that Ray would most likely not move to Colorado in the near future, but stay in Kerrville. How he missed his partner and friend Margie, and how, still to this day, he values our friendship, which now spans twenty-five years.

CHAPTER 31

Union Issues

It was obviously time for drastic measures ...

To Chuck on September 24, 2010

Chuck,

I am fully aware that I need to respond to your last e-mail, but at this moment I could use your counsel. I will do my best to be brief.

Facts:

May 5, 2010: Jack calls in sick for a 10 a.m. children's performance in New Brunswick. Jack is permitted eighteen sick services per season, but he has a history of calling out to some of our run-out gigs.

Who is aware of this history? Has he ever been called on this before? Is there a written track record of this?

I am the keeper of the payroll records, as well as keeping track of all personnel infractions.

Jack plays a Broadway show; let's call it *Jump*. I am on a freelance gig the same night with another musician who also plays *Jump*; let's call her Blondie.

In passing, I asked Blondie how Jack was doing. Blondie told me that Jack had called in sick for the matinee. I was relieved by her answer, because if a musician calls in sick to a service and is caught playing another gig during a scheduled NJSO service, their contract will be terminated on the spot. I mentioned to Blondie this possibility, merely as an informative statement on how our organization operates. I later learned she told Jack that I was checking up on him. With this lie, the floodgates opened.

Do you now Blondie well? Why did she tell Jack?

I cannot imagine why she said anything to Jack. I have known her for more than twenty years. I thought we had a good relationship in place—obviously I was wrong. Blondie told Jack that I asked her about his participation at *Jump* on the day he called in sick—again, this is a bold-faced lie. But why? I am sincerely perplexed over her actions.

The next day, May 6, while at work, Jack approached me. He was furious, hot under the collar, and pissed beyond words. He asked me if I actually asked Blondie if he had gone to play *Jump* the day he called in sick. I told him exactly what happened, and how Blondie and I were playing the same gig. Jack had come up in conversation, but I never asked if he had been to *Jump* the same day. Clearly Jack did not believe what I was saying. He was livid and felt that I had betrayed him.

Mistake! Your conversations with his colleagues are none of his bloody business.

How did he find out that you had asked? Had to be Blondie, no? Watch her!

As personnel manager, it is my prerogative (and obligation) to unearth deceptions. It is also acceptable to ask a player who calls in sick for a doctor's note. I understand that when Jack found out I spoke to Blondie, it appeared to be something that it wasn't.

Three months passed. It is now August 25, when I received a letter from Local 802 in New York City. They were accusing me of violating a fellow musicians' character. This is a member-to-member complaint, *not* personnel manager to musician—impossible!

Unacceptable definition of the problem. It doesn't matter what 802 wants to call it, this is only a matter of an orchestra manager fulfilling his professional obligations to his orchestra colleagues and to his administration. There is nothing whatsoever personal involved, and you can't discuss it on that basis.

I absolutely agree. It is none of 802's business at all. I am sure of this. The way I see it is, Jack missed his grievance period with the NJSO. He and Blondie work together and must have been talking about this for weeks on end. During this time, they devised a plan in which to get even with me. I can't imagine how this must have festered, all the while growing bigger than life.

I responded to 802, offering the collective bargaining agreement of the NJSO and Local 16 (who governs our organization), stating that in our organization a musician has fifteen days to file a grievance. I later learned that Jack had filed the grievance in New York because the New York union allows grievances to be filed up to two years after an incident.

Okay. Not stupid.

I included that portion of our CBA to 802, nothing more.

Long and the short of it is, 802 will hold a hearing on October 12 to determine if I was negligent in my treatment of Jack via Blondie. I told 802 they had no jurisdiction over this matter. I explained that Jack is angry over this misunderstanding, not over any 802 issue. I also told them I would not attend such a hearing. I learned today that 802 will hold a hearing with or without me, and the outcome will be final. Honestly, Chuck, most of me really does not care about the insecurities of Jack, but the other part knows that I did not do anything wrong.

Of course you didn't—Blondie did. What are the possible outcomes of the 802 meeting, with or without you?

After reading the 802 rules and bylaws, I found this:

1. Reprimand the accused; and/or
2. Assess a fine, in accordance with these bylaws; and/or
3. Suspend or expel him or her from membership in the Union, or accord such other penalty as is consistent with these bylaws.

I spoke with the Local 16 council, and understand that I am permitted to not show up at the hearing, but I am able to respond with a written statement. Here is my question. If I do so, am I not saying that 802 has precedence over the NJSO and Local 16? Why answer these allegations? See my letter, below.

That depends. Also—you might confer with Local 16.

I have Local 16 on board. Now I need to contact the symphony attorney.

They might tell New York City that they have no jurisdiction and should get lost.

That is certainly possible, but Local 802, under their bylaws, *must* hold the hearing and decide on an outcome. The outcome could be "Case dismissed." I have no way of knowing until it is over.

If I do not answer, surely I will lose the hearing as a "no show" or "no evidence." On the other hand, if I write a complete response, I am allowing Jack his way.

Not necessarily—he is accusing you improperly and unjustly, and you have an obligation to defend yourself and your orchestra.

Furthermore, if I respond, I must respond as the personnel manager of the NJSO, because that is how this entire matter originated. If this is the origination point, 802 *has no jurisdiction.*

I don't understand—why does 802 have no jurisdiction?

Local 802 has no jurisdiction over this matter because it has to do with my position as personnel manager here in New Jersey, not the freelance gig where Blondie and I spoke.

Have you told your boss about this?

Of course, I told her everything—I informed her last May when this all took place.

Here is the letter I would like you to read, and offer your thoughts:

> Dear Local 802:
> Thank you for your correspondence, and for the information relative to the unfortunate matter that Jack has chosen to bring before you.
>
> After consulting with the New Jersey Symphony Orchestra's attorney, President of Local 16 AFM, General Manager of the

NJSO and against my better judgment as a contractor of 25 years and personnel manager of the NJSO for the past eight seasons, we have collectively come to this conclusion: It is not possible to address this issue without answering any questions as the Personnel Manager of the NJSO.

I am being accused of wrongdoings by Jack for simply doing my job—it is my prerogative and obligation to use whatever means necessary to help make my organization run smoothly.

I respectfully decline further statement.
Sincerely,
Jim Neglia

That is where I am at this point. I would like to include some variation of a letter to present to Local 802 and put this matter to rest. I am sick of it. Thanks for your continued support. I am sure you have better things to do than read this nonsense.

The letter is good. Seek approval from the NJSO council.

From Chuck on October 12, 2010
I hope that you all are okay. So? What happened?

To Chuck on October 13, 2010
Boss,
You are good, and I mean really good! Shows your depth, love, and understanding, remembering yesterday was the trial. I love you for caring, helping, and giving a darn!

Hey! My mind is not gone yet!

I received a call from Local 802 at 11:20 the morning of the trial. (It was a 10:30 hearing. At first they were attempting to be so strong. "This is Local 802 looking for James Neglia."

"Yes, how can I help you?"

"We are holding a hearing—where are you?"

I asked them if they received my response six weeks ago displaying the NJSO policy and timeline for grievance procedure. They did not. I asked, "Did you receive a letter from the president of Local 16 (NJSO Union), stating that Local 802 was breaking the law of the National Labor Union by filing such charges from member to management? They responded no.

It was obvious: Local 802's higher-ups never forwarded my letters and Local 16's e-mails to the trial board.

No kidding? How could you tell? Bunch of chicken-gutted dicks! Didn't even have the cojones to stand up and do what they thought that they should be doing.

The trial board told me that they would call me right back. I never received a call.

That's worse! I have no patience with that kind of gutless, unprofessional BS!

I am done with this nonsense. I spoke with my general manager this evening at about 7:00 p.m. and suggested we—the complainant, orchestra committee chair, general manager, personnel manager and a mediator— hold a meeting to resolve this and parallel issues. I hope this will help the situation and put an end to this insanity.

Good move.

I am sure that a member of our orchestra committee gave very bad advice to the complainant, causing further problems.

Sounds probable—didn't he have to go through the committee before he filed a gripe?

It is my intention to spill what I know when we are all together in a room with a mediator. I am 100 percent sure that a member of our very own orchestra committee advised Jack to go to Local 802, not realizing this is an absolute violation of the National Labor Union (article 8121b), which states in part that a member cannot file such cause against management for following guidelines of their job.

Okay. But may I make a suggestion? These boobs know for sure that they screwed up and embarrassed themselves. Not a bad idea to do this in the meeting, but maybe it's a good idea to do it in a way that suggests that you are really upset that there was so much misinformation out there—a really poor situation almost developed because a few people, who shall remain nameless, didn't understand and violated the bylaws of Local 16. Tch tch, such a shame. I hope that all parties understand now how things should be done. Your point will have been made, you will not have fried anyone's privates in public and made enemies, and you are Mr. Good Guy.

By offering this information, the orchestra committee member is in violation of the bylaws of Local 16. You know the old saying: give someone enough rope, and you know what will happen.

(Unreal situation. Yeah. Usually they will try and hang you.

As for the rest, I am happy to have kept such good notes on this issue, and the chapter is nearly complete.

Absolutely. It should be a matter of record. You never know what some jerk will do next week.

I am off to work. Be well and as always. It is wonderful hearing from you.

Ditto. I hope that Sasha and the boys are in good shape.

Follow-up e-mail a few days later:
Chuck,

You might want to grab a cup of coffee … Long and short of it is that Local 16 *and* their lawyers discouraged me from attending the 802 trial board meeting. Local 802 held the trial without me. Their findings were this: I violated some article of the 802 union, which is punishable in one of three ways. They the least of the three. The large complaint and violation was dismissed altogether.

Have you discussed this with the Local 16 people?

Bottom line is the attorney for Local 16 insists on me filing a complaint against Local 802 for violating the National Labor Union rule (article 81b1). This article basically shields me in my managerial position. In a nutshell, it states that one union cannot levy charges against a member of another union for doing one's job, even if someone doesn't like how I do my job.

Bravi! That sounds appropriate and right!

I have prepared my written statement (see below) and will present it to the National Labor Union, who has an office in Newark. I will file next week when I have some time on my hands.

You may ask why I am doing this. I have an answer for you. I feel if I don't, 802 will do this to someone else, and the snowball will continue. I will not be any part of that type of destruction.

Absolutely right. There is an old German expression: "For the insult, draw the sword!" Besides, their position is just dead-wrong and extreme—this running-nose jerk sounds like he has a guilty conscience.

Most I can win is for 802 to be humiliated, dismiss all charges, write a letter of apology to me, and inform the original person who complained that the case has been dismissed due to negligence on the part of Local 802.

Yes, that would be nice—and the right thing to do. But there is no reason to believe that they will do it.

Screw it, it is worth it in my eyes. It will cost me nothing, but it can offer me some muscle once the story begins to circulate.

Yes, it is very important that everyone knows that you take no nonsense—and this is nonsense!—from anyone, including the big powerhouse unions.

When you can, let me know what you think.

Sending good thoughts to you!

My letter to begin the complaint against Local 802 with the Labor Union:

> National Labor Relations Board,
>
> I, James Neglia, herewith file official charges against Local 802 for violating article 8B1B of the National Labor Union laws.
>
> I am the Orchestra Personnel Manager of the New Jersey

Symphony Orchestra (NJSO) as well as a member of Local 802 Musicians Union in New York City, and Local 16 in New Jersey. Local 16 is the presiding local with whom the NJSO has filed our collective bargaining agreement (CBA).

On August 20, 2010 I received a complaint from Local 802 on behalf of member Jack. (Exhibit A.) It is due to this complaint that I am seeking your help.

Here are the events which took place on May 5 and 6, 2010:

NJSO member Jack called in sick on the morning of May 5 for a children's concert in New Brunswick, New Jersey. I excused him in the same manner I have done for any and every member of the Symphony who calls in sick. That is to say, "Feel better and I will see you tomorrow unless I hear otherwise." Musicians of the NJSO are permitted 18 sick services per year.

Later that same evening, I met Blondie Mae on a freelance gig in Newark. Being that both Jack and Blondie play *Jump* in New York City, I asked Blondie how Jack was doing. Blondie told me that earlier in the day, Jack had called in sick for the matinee. I told her that he had also called in sick for the symphony service in the morning, and that I hoped that he was feeling better.

The next morning, May 6, 2010, the NJSO was performing in Englewood, New Jersey, at another children's service. Jack approached me, quivering, shaking and nearly unable to speak. I asked him if he was okay, and what it was that I could help him with. He asked me what right I had asking about him to his colleague Blondie. I told him that I saw her, knew that they worked together, and inquired as to how he was feeling, nothing more. Jack then told me that I had no right to ask about his non-NJSO time. I did say to Jack that I am permitted to ask questions about players as I see fit. This is my duty and obligation as Personnel Manager of the NJSO.

As a result of Blondie's insensitivities and of her malicious act, she singlehandedly has tainted Jack's relationship with me, and in turn, Jack has tainted my NJSO working environment. This has snowballed into a situation which could have cost me my job, unjustly and viciously defamed my professional reputation and my character, and sent rumors flying at my place of employment, where tensions now are exaggerated.

On August 19, 2010, some 108 days later, Local 802 member Jack filed a *member-on-member* complaint with Local 802. (Exhibit A.)

On August 25, 2010, I responded to the letter *as the Personnel Manager of the NJSO*, not as Jim Neglia, the freelance percussionist and contractor. (Exhibit B.) I outlined the grievance process clearly for Local 802 to digest.

On September 20, 2010, I received a letter from Local 802 (Exhibit C) instructing me to appear before the trial board of Local 802. Reflecting on my position in the matter, I could not see how I could separate Neglia the Personnel Manager of the NJSO from Neglia the accused.

When Local 802 informed me that they were holding a hearing to decide whether or not I had been in violation of their outlined rules, I knew that I needed assistance. As a union member, I called the president of Local 16 to seek advice. I was then referred to Mr. Seymour Heckman. Mr. Heckman is a member of Pratt-Heckman, LLC, attorneys at law.

In the interim, the president of Local 16 prepared and sent a letter to Local 802 on my behalf. (Exhibit D.)

This letter informs Local 802 that they have no jurisdiction over a NJSO (Local 16) issue. Local 802 ignored the letter and proceeded with their hearing. The result of their trial is included as Exhibit E. I believe that my rights have been violated, and have decided to pursue this matter to the fullest extent permitted by law.

I am seeking a written apology from Local 802 regarding the entire matter. In addition, Local 802 must send a letter to member Jack, informing him that the trial board of Local 802 had broken the rules of the National Labor Union and with that, all charges and verdicts against me have been dismissed.

Both Mr. Heckman and I understand that Article 8b1b is a very obscure article, perhaps rarely used or challenged. However, Mr. Heckman requests that if you have any question concerning this matter or article, to contact him.

Respectfully submitted,
James Neglia
Orchestral Personnel Manager
New Jersey Symphony Orchestra

Good letter. The only problem is that even if they do eradicate the trial and verdict, they still haven't erased the record of the improper charges, have they? The accusations should be withdrawn. What does Mr. Heckman say? Onward and upward!

November 5, 2010

Chuck,
Thank you for taking the time out to respond so thoroughly, I sincerely appreciate it.

Hey, come on—it's me, not some stranger!

I am always concerned with the possibility of things heading south, but do not think there can or will be any serious ramifications, regardless of the final outcome.

Hey, life is hard, and there is always a possibility things don't resolve as planned, especially when you deal with obviously misguided people.

If Jack gets black and blue from the Labor Union, he has no one but Local 802 to blame. In the final analysis, 802 did decide to give his pissing and moaning their attention. And if 802 winds up with egg on their face, I don't think there will be any repercussions for me here in New Jersey whatsoever.

Not if they use their heads.

President of Local 16 and Heckman are squarely behind me, and are really pushing for a complaint to be filed.

Good. It is a potentially serious breach of decorum and procedures on 802's part.

Heckman worked for the National Labor Union for fifteen-plus years and still does as a consultant. This guy knows his stuff! He has asked me to bypass Local 16 and to work directly with him. This is unprecedented behavior for the legal representative of Local 16, to cut them out in order to work with a member directly. I asked Heckman about it and why he wanted to operate in such a manner. Ray told me that involving Local 16 might complicate the complaint. Local 16 will still be paying for his services. Win-win situation all around.

Sounds right. Bravo!

I made the changes in my statement to the labor union as you suggested—many thanks. I am sure they will ask me many questions and have me sign a sworn affidavit. Once submitted, I am sure it will take at least six months before I hear anything at all. Honestly, I don't care. I just refuse to roll over and go away.

Absolutely. Weakness attracts attacks and disrespect.

See, you taught me well!

You have the right instincts. Don't give any, don't take any—crap, that is! How is Sasha with all of this ka-ka?

If I may ... Even after all these years, I am still overwhelmed by your kindness, generosity, and caring, loving spirit.

Don't be—that is what ancient friends do.

You always take the time to help me, always.

Of course. I am happy that in some small way that I am able.

I selfishly ask your advice, fully knowing it will take a considerable amount of energy to respond.

There is nothing selfish about it—we go back a long way. And if I didn't want to do it, you would hear it in a hurry!

Regardless, you never let me down. I selfishly state my case, talking about my accomplishments, problems, issues, and family, leaving a few sparse lines to inquire about you and yours. I have a lot to learn; don't stop teaching me.

Forget that word "selfish," will you? I am here! Happiness to you all. Onward and upward!

Chuck, for your entertainment, here is the 802 ruling.

Disposition of the Trial Board in Case of Jack vs. James Neglia—Case #112

The Local 802 Trial Board was convened on September 20, 2010, at 10:00 a.m. at Local 802 to conduct a Procedural Review of the case of Jack vs. Neglia; present at that time were X, Y, and Z, which constituted a quorum of the Board.

After reviewing the charges and discussing procedural matters, the Board voted unanimously that the case should in fact be tried, and set a Trial date of October 12, 2010.

The Local 802 Trial Board was re-convened on October 12, 2010, at 10:30 a.m. at Local 802 to try the case of Jack vs. Neglia; present at that time were X, Y, and Z, which constituted a quorum of the Board. Also present at that time were Plaintiff Jack and Witness Blondie Mae; Defendant Jim Neglia chose not to appear.

The Board reviewed procedural matters in light of the Defendant's choice to not appear for the trial and consulted with 802 attorneys prior to proceeding. The Board then proceeded to receive testimony from the Plaintiff Jack and the witness Blondie Mae.

The fact pattern *[they are assuming that everything outlined was factual]* outlined in the Plaintiffs "Specifications for charges against Jim Neglia" document was confirmed in oral testimony by the Plaintiff and the Witness. *[I dare them to submit a transcript to you for validation—your word is as good as theirs.]* On May 5 of 2010 Plaintiff Jack called in sick to Defendant (and personnel manager) Neglia for a morning concert of the New Jersey Symphony. Neglia (in the capacity of performing colleague) *[You obviously were not acting in the capacity of "performing colleague" but as the orchestra manager.]* later asked Witness Mae at a rehearsal that evening whether Jack was present at a matinee performance earlier that day of a show where she and Jack were both employed. She responded in the negative, at which point the Defendant allegedly commented that he thought that Jack would have been present at that matinee performance, implying that his sick call that morning might have been disingenuous. *[It implies no such thing. Who has a guilty conscience here?]*

Although there were further conversations between the various parties, some of which involved unpleasantness, the verdict rendered in this trial was based primarily on Neglia's implication as expressed to mutual colleague Mea that Jack's morning sick leave call might not have been honestly made. *[That is one interpretation.]* This cast potential aspersions on Jack's character, and was further aggravated by later exchanges between the parties. On the basis of this primary occurrence, the Trial Board found the Defendant Guilty by unanimous vote under 802 Bylaw IV.1.gg. The additional charge under 802 Bylaw IV.1.ii was dismissed by unanimous vote. The penalty was determined by unanimous vote to be via letter of reprimand, as follows:

Having found Mr. James Neglia guilty of violating Article IV, Section 1, paragraph gg of the By-laws of Local 802, the Trial Board had to choose among three levels of possible penalty. We have chosen to issue this reprimand, the lowest level of penalty, in the hopes that it will be sufficient to stop Mr. Neglia from engaging in all inappropriate, disrespectful and improper behavior toward any member of Local 802. *[You do not recognize their reprimand nor the claimed existence of inappropriate, disrespectful,* *and improper behavior on your part. The only grounds that they have here is possibly your having made any comments about the matter to this creep Mae. As orchestra manager you have every right and responsibility to investigate any suspicion that you have about improprieties on the part of orchestra employees.]*From testimony heard at the trial of Mr. Neglia, it was made clear to the Board that Mr. Neglia's dealings with 802 members Jack and Blondie Mae in the matter of Jack's use of sick days were rife with all of the above. *[Their opinion—paranoia?]* It is wholly unacceptable for a member of Local 802 to address another member of Local 802, whether in the guise of a management representative or as a colleague, with such wanton disregard both for the rights and reputation of the other member and for the protections offered all members by Local 802's By-laws. *[That is an inaccurate and extremist position on the whole matter.]* Mr. Neglia's unwarranted initiation of an investigation into NJSO member Jack's sick-day use and Mr. Neglia's comments to Ms. Mae in the course of that investigation appear to the Board as extremely improper and inflammatory. *[That is their opinion.]* The Board condemns all such behavior and fervently hopes that this behavior will cease immediately. If the Trial Board is reconvened on account of further such occurrences, the higher levels of penalty available may be deemed appropriate at that time. *[Threats are improper and unacceptable and ignored. Are players required to provide any proof of illness severe enough to cause them to miss an obligation?]*

Local 802 Trial Board

In a nutshell, a lot of time and energy was exhorted with little to no outcome at all. What a real shame it ever happened in the first place.

CHAPTER 32

Collapse

Journal Entry: February 23, 2009

About a month ago, I landed myself in the hospital. I nearly passed out during the semifinal round of our principal oboe auditions. Somewhere around candidate number seven, I began to lose control. I went to speak with the committee and informed them that I needed to leave immediately. Fortunately due to our contract language, I had hired four members of the orchestra to assist during the audition process. My colleague Jonathan was able to take over my duties while maintaining his own. I was barely able to drive home without crashing into the guard rail on the highway. When I finally arrived, I went directly to bed for some much-needed rest. It was 5:30 p.m. on Tuesday, January 20.

The finals were scheduled to take place on January 21 from 10 a.m. to 2 p.m. I called my boss and informed her of my situation and instability. Then I did something I had never done before: I took the first sick day of my career. She was able to facilitate the finals in my absence. At 4:00 p.m. of the same day, the full orchestra was scheduled to start a new series. The music we were to perform on this series was Ravel's *Daphnis* and *Chloe Suite 1 and 2*. Both suites required a very large orchestra, which required a more-than-normal amount of concentration and care.

I had taken the morning audition session off, providing me some additional rest. I thought it would be best to stay in bed and rest as much as possible. I wanted to be as strong as I could be before heading to work with the hundred or so musicians hired for the Ravel. I slept until one o'clock and then slowly got up out of bed. I showered, had a cup of coffee, and prepared for the rehearsal ahead. What a mistake I made. I arrived at the hall at around 3:00 p.m. and began to set up the percussion section. Afterward, I placed rosters on the musicians' board, as well as on stage right and left, keeping to my normal routine. It was too much for me to handle, and I was beginning to feel the effects.

I made it to about to 4:45 p.m. before dizziness overtook me. I was unable to stand any longer and plopped myself into my waiting chair. I remained still for a few minutes, gathering my strength to keep going. I barely made it to the orchestra break. When that break came, I handed the personnel manager's baton over to my able assistant. I summoned my wife, who was also on stage, and asked her to take me home. She didn't take me home; instead, she took me directly to St. Barnabas Medical Center so I could be helped.

We arrived just before 6:00 p.m., signed in, and took a seat in the waiting room. By 6:30 I was unable to keep my head above my shoulders—the pain was excruciating. When this happened and my wife explained that the pain was generated from my head, I was taken in right away and was tested for everything under the sun. Slowly but surely, all the test results began to come back; all were negative. The tending physician ordered a CT scan. The results were much like the rest of the tests, negative results. A few hours after the CT scan and monitoring, there was little more to do. With a prescription in hand, the hospital released me. It was now just before 1:00 a.m.

While in the hospital, the nurses pumped me with Dilaudid, as well as an anti-sickness drip. I hate medication but took the intravenous drugs because my head was spinning uncontrollably. I was dealing with the most unbearable, piercing pain I had ever experienced. I was still in a fog when the hospital released me. As we were leaving, the doctors told Sasha that I was as strong as an ox, and they were perplexed as to my condition. "Go home and rest," was their prescription, along with the pain medication.

The next morning our (unpublished) home phone rang at 7:30 a.m. It was the head neurologist from St. Barnabas. Apparently, a small spot went unnoticed the night before, but now on the CT scan, it had surfaced. The neurologist was concerned that it could be an aneurism. They strongly suggested that I return to undergo an MRI immediately. I explained that I had just taken five hundred milligrams of Percocet and was in no condition to move. After a few seconds of thought, I got up, dressed, and headed back to the hospital.

During the fifteen-minute trip, I was still feeling the effects of the Percocet, as well as the drip medication absorbed hours before. I was completely out of it—couldn't walk, talk, or function at all. I have no real recollection of the trip to hospital that morning.

When I arrived, the doctors were waiting for me. They placed me on a gurney, administered a pain killer drip (most likely Dilaudid), and took me immediately to the MRI room. The drip was now in addition to the effects of the medication of the night before, as well as the Percocet I took an hour earlier. I was flying.

I struggled during the forty-five-minute procedure. I felt that I couldn't breathe. I wanted out, and I wanted out *now*. The MRI took place in three stages, about fifteen minutes each. After the first stage had been completed, I motioned to the attendants that I was finished. "Take me out of here!" I shouted over and over. I felt the padded table begin to move out from the walls that surrounded me. I immediately began to feel better; I was free from the machine and the unbearable volume that surrounded me. Pleading with the technicians not to send me back into that contraption, I was quickly reminded that this was absolutely necessary. An older man looked at me; his face was well defined by years of experience. He spoke with me in a soft, subtle tone and offered me the chance to stop the test, but in the same breath he reminded me that my family needed to see the results. He put his hand on my side and slowly nodded up and down. "It is time to continue, Jim. I will be here to help you." Despite my claustrophobic, drug-induced state, I agreed to continue.

During the next two excruciating segments, I tried to focus on life—my life. Joys and happy times, travels past and trips yet to come. My wife, our kids, our family, brothers, sisters, and all those amazing nieces and nephews. Past performances, upcoming dates, special guests, and ancient greats. I did my best to remain focused, but the cylindrical machine and deafening loudness left me paralyzed. I came face to face with fear itself. Just as I was about to call it all off, I heard the machine being powered down, and a familiar voice spoke. "It is all over, Jim. You made it. Good for you."

For the first time in my life, I thought it just might be my time to check out for good. I don't know if it was the drugs or the extreme pain I experienced, but I definitely recall thinking, *My time may be up.* I remember the sadness that surrounded me, leaving my wife and kids behind, feeling I have so much more to offer. I recall feeling that I needed more time with my wife, more time with my family. There was more to do, more to accomplish. I was honestly scared. During the recovery process, it became clear that I had been given a second chance.

The MRI came back negative: no aneurism, nothing else in view. The baffled doctors began to talk about meningitis. Isn't that nice? More testing, more time under the spell of the drugs, more time consumed with the unknown. After several hours of testing and discussions among the specialists, they had come to a conclusion. The final diagnosis was that I had been suffering from a severe sinus infection. We were grateful that it wasn't something more serious, but I was perplexed as to why it went undetected until now. I lost a full week of work and slept four of those days straight through.

CHAPTER 33

Europe

To Chuck on September 6, 2011
Chuck,
When you send such an e-mail, I have no other choice but to drop everything and write back. Sit back and grab a glass of red.

You got that right! Always ready!

In a nutshell, the trip was wonderful. I am not going to bore you with all the same stories you may hear from so many others; instead, I will share some of my personal favorite experiences and observations.

The absolute highlight of the Amsterdam portion of the trip was seeing Jory. He stayed with us for at least six to seven hours for each of the four days we were in the city. We did everything together—reminisced about Mannes, you, life, music, work, family, immigration process, dual citizenship, and a million other topics. We shared meals, walked in parks, visited museums, and the zoo! We talked and talked. Sasha, Phillip, and Daniel fell in love with him almost immediately, and he with them. What a remarkable guy, exactly as I remembered him back in 1993 during my last visit to Paris. I miss him now, as do my boys, who often ask how is Uncle Jory.

Yep, a real class act and one really good guy.

While in Belgium we hit Bruges (which was our absolute favorite), as well as Antwerp, Brussels and its magnificent square, Zee Bruges, the North Sea (where we went swimming), and Gent.

Must have been a chilly ocean! Wonderful food, fabulous sites. We would go back on the exact trip, same cities, in a heartbeat. Brussels offered us a wonderfully warm feeling, one which carried through on the entire trip.

In Paris we visited all the regular sites in the city and enjoyed all the tasty morsels made available to us. Olive bread made its way to the top of our favorite noshing food quite quickly.

That makes sense.

We shopped in the markets, picked up fresh vegetables, cheeses, salamis, wine, more bread, more olive bread, pickles, and anything else you can think of for a noshing picnic—usually twice daily. We did hit a few restaurants here and there but found it was easier to pick things up along the way.

Good for you—great thing to do. And you ate like Parisians.

The Select Hotel was in such a great location; we rarely needed the bus or underground.

Yep—remember that I stayed there, too?

We took a few bus trips for Daniel to enjoy but basically walked everywhere. From our hotel to the Mont Parness building, to the Eiffel Tower, to Invalides, Montmartre, Sacré Cœur, and beyond.

Bravo! Best way to do it.

As you know, the Pantheon was just a few short blocks away—so many wonderful memories, so many wonderful things to do and see. Daniel said to me, "Papa, I loved Paris the most because everywhere I look, there is something to see." I nearly fell over.

Now that is a kid who knows where it's all at! I have repeatedly said something similar: that everywhere you look in Paris, there is something beautiful to see, and if you don't think that it's beautiful, it will surely be interesting!

Daniel, now seven going on twenty-seven, enjoyed himself more than I thought he would. In eighteen days he never asked when we were going home or back to the hotel. We would leave the hotel after breakfast, about 10:00 a.m., and wouldn't return until about 8:00 p.m., with very little stopping. He tried every food under the sun, from crepes with all sorts of fillings, to escargot, braised lamb, vegetable dishes, frog legs, and other eatables. We were really proud of him!

No kidding? He is an unusual young man—most kids recoil from alien food!

When we would return back to the hotel in Paris, we would take a table in the café adjacent to the Select and remain there until closing, usually about midnight. Sasha and I would then begin to unwind, ordering some soup or croque-madame (another favorite for Daniel), or something green. Then we would open our magic bag and pull out a bottle (or two or three) of some new red we had just purchased up the block. The waiters got to know us pretty quickly and never gave us any problem; we tipped them handsomely.

I used to go there, too!

I brought with me my iPad and was able to use the free Wi-Fi to check in with family and e-mail, to see how things were going. Additionally, I had my iPhone, which I used only once during the entire trip to find Jory. We did use the iPhone when we had free Wi-Fi to "face time" some friends back home, and that was wonderful. I tell you, Chuck; I didn't think about work for one minute; it was a real vacation.

That is the way that it is supposed to be, and from what you write, you did all the right things in the right way. Must be Sasha's influence!

Driving was a blast as well. I love driving, especially a manual car; there's something about a stick shift that makes me feel like I am in control of the vehicle. The drive from Paris back to Amsterdam took longer than I figured, so we decided to stop at some of the more attractive "exits" along the way. One such stop was in Arras, France.

Terrible fighting there in World War I.

It was a cute little town where Sasha added to her European wardrobe in full force. She was happy; I was thrilled for her.

You are a good husband!

The trip did take some unexpected turns here and there, most of which resulted in some sort of financial savings. For instance, when Sasha and I went to Schiphol Airport to pick up our rental car, we were told that we didn't need to rent a car seat for Daniel, a 50€ savings—not so bad! Well, our luck continued. One night while in Bruges, we had ordered a substantial meal that included several nice bottles of wine, mussels to die for, and other tasty dishes. After our meal, I ordered an espresso for myself, and Sasha and asked for the bill. The waiter acknowledged my request and a few minutes later the espresso arrived, but the bill never did. I flagged down the waiter again about ten minutes later with the universal sign for the check. He just waved and smiled. A third time, I called to him but he never came. By this time nearly forty-five minutes had passed from the original time I ordered the espresso. Daniel needed to go to the rest room, so Sasha took him, and Phillip and I waited at the table for a few more minutes. At some point Phillip said, "I have to go to the bathroom as well," and he excused himself. I was the only one who remained at the table. A few more minutes passed, and I needed to relieve myself of the wine and espresso as well, so I went to the restroom. There was no sign of Sasha or Daniel, but Phillip was washing his hands; he told me Mama would be waiting for us upstairs. After doing my business, I went upstairs and saw Sasha looking in a storefront window a few feet away. I assumed the bill was squared away. Long story short, I thought she paid, she thought I paid, and the waiter thought we paid, as we actually bumped into him and he wished us a good night. It wasn't until hours later, while in the comforters of our hotel room, that we realized no one had paid the bill, about €200.

Whoa! Serious bread! That adds to the fun! The waiter must have liked Sasha!

When we pulled up to the Select Hotel, one couldn't help but notice that it was overshadowed by the University of Paris. When we checked in, I enquired about their parking lot. It was then that we learned that parking around the university was free for the month of August in spots marked *"payant."* Another €200 saved. After checking in, I started the car, drove about a hundred meters, and parked the car in that beautiful *payant* spot, not to return for eight days.

Not bad! Did you visit the Sorbonne?

There are more stories like this, but I fear if I go on you would never believe me! Free meals in the Bruges hotel, for instance. I digress; the hotel in Bruges was spectacular in every way you can imagine. The Weinebrugge Hotel is located at the entrance of the peaceful and green environment of the Tillegem Forest. The building itself is set far off the road. The quiet surroundings and fresh, crisp air offered us a fantastic sleep climate, no air-conditioning required. The Weinebrugge is about a ten-minute drive from downtown Bruges. With our short rides back and forth, we were able to enjoy a bit of the countryside. What fabulous surroundings, and the roads were clean as a whistle. Oh, get this: they had king-size beds to boot! Holy cow!

Sounds great, and what a location.

One night we returned after a long day, only to find we hadn't sufficiently stuffed our faces during the day. We ordered some nibble food (cheese platters, fruits, and a pot of mussels in wine and garlic sauce). When the bill came, the wonderfully adorable, little old waitress asked us if we would like to have the charge placed on our hotel bill. We agreed, but when we left a few days later, the charge never appeared. I mean, come on! About €90 saved.

Life sometimes surprises us.

When we returned the car after our long journey from Paris back to Schiphol, we were about eight hours past our drop off time. We were never billed for the additional time, not even a prorated expense! I don't get it, €75 per day minimum, no?

(Somebody somewhere was watching out for you guys!

If we would have stayed any longer, the trip may have paid us back! No, just joking. The actual cost was right about where I thought, and I have zero regrets making the expense. Daniel talks about Europe all the time, and he wants to go to Italy next. Remarkable young man; I am so proud of him.

You should be. He will go absolutely ape in Italy!

As for me, eighteen days went by too quickly.

Always does.

I had a difficult time making the transition back to the States. I have always felt like part of me really belongs in Europe.

I couldn't agree more. I too felt that way—still do! I always felt very comfortable. Perhaps one day, Sasha and I will spend a longer period of time exploring and feeling the culture of wherever we may find ourselves. Traveling with her is a true blessing, something I never experienced in my past life. She was helping to navigate our way from country to country, side street to side street—something that made me feel so very comfortable. She had the boys relaxed and prepared every step of the way, while discussing the next day's events with me the night before. I can talk about her, our relationship, our children, and our successes and commitments to you and anyone else who would listen all night long.

Man, you'd better be grateful, because that is pretty rare and very valuable!

Mannes was another blessing. From a young age I began to understand people, connections, caring, and more. I met some friends in the early eighties who are with me to this day.

That is about as valuable as it gets!

At the top of the list is you. I can tell you this: Phillip (seventeen) knows you well, as does Sasha. I speak of you often, using your example, teachings, and guidance, which I can hopefully pass along to my sons.

And that, for me, is as valuable as it gets! Kind words that I am happy to hear.

He understands what commitment means; the same for dedication, determination, and focus. He is also learning, albeit slowly, what it means to be punctual.

I often remind Phillip of how you and I would share a few stories, a cup of coffee, and a bagel while you attacked the *New York Times* crossword each morning before 7:00 a.m.!

Those were good days.

I could go on, but anything I would say to you would be redundant.

You're a good man, Chuck, and I am proud to have you all these years in my life.

And if I didn't feel the same way about you, we wouldn't have the relationship.

So, where to next? Working on saving some funds once we pay off the rest of the Sapphire card.

Of course, and then start saving for the Naples-Rome-Florence-Siena-Milan-Venice orbit! Right?

All is well in our home; we are blessed in every sense of the word.

You deserve it! Great travel story; thank you! Happiness to you all.

CHAPTER 34

Má Vlast

*Playing my instrument is the ultimate escape, a trancelike state
that always diverts my attention from everything else around me*

—The Author

Journal Entry: December 22, 2001

I was in Manhattan by 4:00 p.m., where I was to meet my nephew
Michael (age fourteen) at Lincoln Center. He is in the Julliard Orchestra
Preparatory division and had a dress rehearsal he wanted me to hear.
Michael was my pride and joy, my nephew, and my number-one student.
From a very early age, he possessed great talent in music, showing
versatility, specifically on the snare drum and timpani. His hands were
mature for his young age, and his perfect pitch was an asset to anyone
in his position.

I needed to be at St. Patrick's by 5:30 p.m. to prepare for my own
rehearsal. I listened to him for a little while, enjoying his wonderful
sense of timing, rhythm, and pitch. He was playing timpani on *Moldau*
by Bedřich Smetana. I listened fully with undivided attention to his
rehearsal, feeling the placement of every timpani stroke. As the time
came when I needed to run to my rehearsal, I caught Mike's eye, sent a
short wave of, "Okay, sounds fine," and headed out the door.

I had enough time to walk across town to Fifty-first and Madison. I took
the brisk walk, all the while deep in thought. I was reliving the short
rehearsal I had just attended, recalling each and every stroke produced

by my young and budding nephew. I picked up my cell and called Mike so we could talk more about his performance. By the time I called, his rehearsal had finished, and he was going out to dinner with his friends. We chatted about his rehearsal and what he could do over the next few hours to improve his eight o'clock performance. Mostly he appeared to be nervous, and I felt the need to talk him down.

Having finished my rehearsal closer to 8:00 p.m. than I had hoped for, I hailed a cab from the east side and made my way back to Lincoln Center. I hoped I would be able to make it back for the performance of the Smetana, which was slated to open the program. With the luck from the gods above who help decide on certain New York traffic routes, I made it for the opening.

I took my seat, and so it began. Smetana's symphonic poem "Má Vlast" was composed in 1874 and portrays the river called the Moldau as a kind of rondo, with the flowing theme of the river recurring in different forms between colorful episodes depicting Bohemian life and folklore along the riverside. One can hear Smetana's yearning for his fatherland. The music is filled with hope, longing, and lots of emotions. It opens with two flutes in a pattern that is intertwined and engaging. This is followed by the theme played in the string section. The principal theme rang out in a lush, rich sound produced by the violins, punctuated by the timpani with my nephew steering the ship.

The piece continues with a sailor's march into the voyage home to "My Fatherland." My heart was filled with joy and passion. Unable to hold back my own emotions, I cried a heavy cry, the kind where it was hard to catch my breath. I could only imagine what the people next to me were thinking. I was emotional for several reasons. I had been to the Czech Republic more than a dozen times, and I had adopted it, as well as my friends and acquaintances there, as my home away from home. I wanted to go back. I wanted to see my friends and family so far away. Along with this was the sight and sound of my number-one student leading the forces behind the tonic and dominant. At that moment, it was all too much for me to digest.

During these twelve minutes of sheer joy, I began to think about them—all of them, my Czech family and how I missed them. With the holidays approaching, I felt the separation grow even deeper, and the haunting melody of the *Moldau* brought me to tears and more sorrow. It also reminded me of my deeper understanding of the commitment to my true love, the constant in my life—music. Friends and families both here and afar became my strong focus: keep love alive in your heart and fear nothing. As Smetana's passion is for his Fatherland, I have found mine is in my life of music.

CONCLUSION

And in the End …

Reviewing the stories that I shared in the pages of this book allows me to reflect in amazement at some of the most incredible events that ultimately shaped my life. I paused and reflected on each of the passages, thinking about what could have been, if only one part of any particular event had gone differently. What would I be doing today if I hadn't taken that phone call on Sixty-sixth Street, or witnessed touring disarray overseas? What would I be doing if I wasn't introduced to Karl Haas more than forty years ago? Where would I be if not for my travels overseas and my love of Europe? How would I feel about work if I chose a different path, one other than in the arts?

I am forced to think about how many times I didn't know how I would manage myself as a musician. How would I come through and produce without being crushed under the stronghold of my art, and the burden that accompanied it? Could I sustain my desire to succeed? Could I push as hard as required, and if so, for how long? I was challenged at every crossroad, thoughts gripping my mind. Was I making the right choice? I had so many questions, all with endless possibilities and all with very different outcomes. It is daunting to think how many times I could have screwed thing up; irreparable damage was just one bad choice away. Somehow I avoided huge catastrophes, but I found myself putting out smaller fires along the way.

In the early years, determination and desire were a large part of the equation that helped to move me forward. However, what I learned many years later was that there was one other very important element added to the mix: passion. As I grew, first as a person and later as a percussionist, personnel manager, husband, and father, I witnessed my strong desires to move forward with what can only be described as passion. Once I realized this was the missing (or unfocused) piece of the puzzle, everything in my life began to crystallize and become much more intense. It was a real phenomenon at the time. Once recognized, I was able to quickly incorporate all the elements of passion into my daily life and goals. As passion took a stronghold in my life and as I began to understand and harness all its wonderful offerings, I began to feel unstoppable in all I pursued. As a direct result of harnessing the power of passion, I became a better musician, performer, contractor, and person.

In my life, where now I know nothing but happiness, joy, and gratitude, I am grateful to all who have prepared me for this passage. It has been a fantastic journey, one filled with the obvious as well as utter surprise, with joy and tears, with hopes and fears—none of which I would change for a single moment. I have been blessed many times over in ways I have stated in the pages presented before you. I am blessed in so many ways by the inspiration of others, perseverance of all, and the universal language of music, my chosen art form. I am grateful to all the people who have helped me on my life journey. To borrow a phrase from my "ancient friend," I leave you with one great thought.

Onward and Upward!

ABOUT THE AUTHOR

Jim Neglia is a veteran force in the Performing Arts. He has been a working percussionist as well as music contractor, personnel manager and music coordinator for more than 25 years, working closely with some of the best-known names in the industry. Jim covers the entire gamut of music production and performance.

Jim resides in East Hanover, New Jersey with his wife Alexandra, and sons Phillip and Daniel. For relaxation, Jim enjoys traveling, reading, writing and keeping his website, www.JimNeglia.com up to date.

CPSIA information can be obtained at www.ICGtesting.com
Printed in the USA
BVOW021341311212

309453BV00001B/42/P